# BEER SCHOOL

**DRINK YOURSELF CLEVER***

## A CRASH COURSE IN CRAFT BEER

# JONNY GARRETT AND BRAD EVANS

*DRINK RESPONSIBLYISH

Editor: Hugo Villabona
Theme and Layout: Roberto Núñez
Illustrations: Brad Evans
Photography: Brad Evans & Jonny Garrett
Additional photographs: Matt Curtis

ISBN: 978-1-63353-368-4

SOME MAY TAKE

# BEER

**·** TOO **·**

# SERIOUSLY

BUT

# FEW WHO DO ARE

# GUILTY OF TAKING

# LIFE

# TOO SERIOUSLY

# CONTENTS

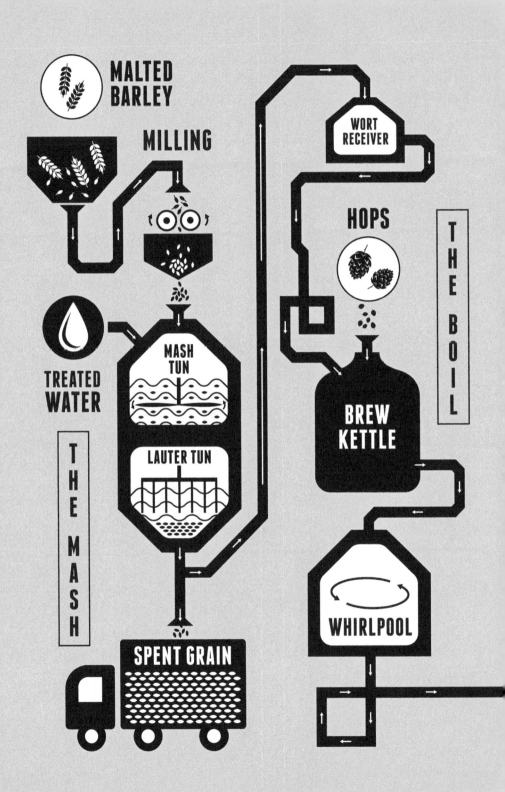

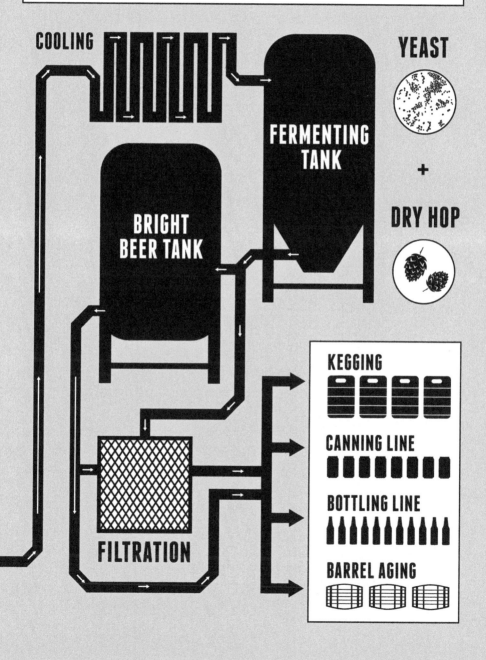

# THE BREWING PROCESS

COOLING

YEAST

FERMENTING TANK

+

DRY HOP

BRIGHT BEER TANK

KEGGING

CANNING LINE

BOTTLING LINE

FILTRATION

BARREL AGING

# CHAPTER

This book is about a journey – about the pursuit of something perfect. As I write this, two friends and I are speeding past New York on Interstate 95. From the cramped backseat, I watch the city lights wink at me invitingly. It's a strange feeling to see Manhattan and not be destined there. No tourist drives past New York. But our journey goes way past it.

We're headed to a farm outside Springfield, Massachusetts, where a brewery called Treehouse is reinventing IPA in the most unlikely setting. The farm where they brew is a long drive from where we were in Philadelphia that morning. Even once you're off the freeway it's a 30-minute meander through towns and country lanes. My friends are skeptical it's worth the drive, but I know it will be.

I want to find out how Treehouse makes beers so fruity, so smooth and so enticing that people come from all over the world to queue for a few cans. I want them to prove to me that one IPA can be so different that it towers over all others. And then I want to know why. I'm not really expecting answers, though; beer is rarely that simple.

The more Brad and I learn about brewing, the more we realise we know nothing. We've spent years reading about, talking about and drinking beer together. We've interviewed everyone from the heads of macro-lager breweries to some dude making gruit out of his shed in the Arctic Circle. All they've managed to do is confuse us even more.

It's disorientating how deep the rabbit hole goes, but that's what makes beer the best drink on earth. Most people take it for granted, but it is one of the most important technological and philosophical accomplishments of the human race. Since being discovered by accident some 6,000 years ago, beer has been credited with inspiring the first biological engineering project, the practice of large-scale crop cultivation, and even a medical advance as an important antibiotic. Some historians think it was part of the formation of society itself.

Clearly these guys don't drink in the same dives that we do, but the point is clear – beer matters. Beer is culture, and its evolution has followed the peaks and troughs of our species, nearly dying out thanks to financial crashes and world wars, before being revived in boom times as part of a worldwide flavour crusade. Beer is as diverse and exciting as the people who drink it. Just like biology, anthropology and the Kardashians, everything you learn about it raises more questions.

At its most basic, brewing is a science; a formula with rights and wrongs. Brewers have spent millennia trying to control natural fermentation to the point where we can break the process down into chemistry – numbers, symbols and equations on a page.

At its most complicated, though, brewing is unfathomable. If it is a science, then it is more akin to alchemy. For all our knowledge, making consistently delicious beer is a desperately difficult task. You can see it in the fact that the truly great brewers of the world – the Cantillons, Russian Rivers, Treehouses – attain a mythical status in the mind of beer hunters like us. And the brewers buy into it too. The owner of a fantastic Italian Lambic brewery once refused to take my praise, claiming it was nature and not him that made the beer so fantastic. Even for those who seek to control it all, religion, superstition and luck have a vital part in beer's history and its future.

At first humans put their brewing faith in the gods, praying to Ninkasi (the ancient Sumerian goddess of beer) and then fermenting grain in the same pots, believing them blessed. Now we know that using the same pots worked by inadvertently cultivating the same yeast. But brewers still have their favourite fermenters or unwavering belief in "first-wort hopping." Through repetition and recording results, two things brewers have to be very good at, that favour turns into understanding, and faith turns into knowledge.

Speaking of knowledge, you possibly don't know what first-wort hopping is. The truth is that I didn't until relatively recently. But you'll know exactly what it is, along with endless other vital bits of information, by the end of this book. The aim of Beer School is to take you on the same journey that beer has gone through, whether that's literally through the pipes of a brewhouse or through the chronicles of time. All the while, we'll pick apart the science from the art of brewing, using our experiences and those of some of the world's greatest brewers.

But we're not going to stop there, because the journey doesn't either. Understanding beer is vital to enjoying it – not only how it's brewed but how it should be stored, served and drunk. We're going to get totally lost in all that – what glassware, what temperatures, and how to pour. It's not being precious or nerdy to say that tiny decisions can massively change how we perceive flavour. After all the hard work that went into brewing, we should do the brewer justice.

What happens to the beer after it leaves the brewery is almost as important as what happens before. A beer's journey doesn't end until you've drunk it, smiled and reached for another. Each one is another step towards enlightenment. And so is every chapter in this book. Welcome to Beer School, the best days of your life.

# CHAPTER

# GREAT
# BEER
# STARTS WITH
## AN
# IDEA

All beers start in a brewer's head. It could be a craving for grapefruit, a weird idea about peanuts, or the ambition to make the best pilsner ever. Their skill as a brewer is how he or she translates that ambition into liquid.

But before we get to that we must recognize that the original idea has to be a great one. Even if no one else thinks it's great, that conviction and clarity of concept is hugely important. This is the first lesson in brewing.

When you look back at the breweries that have made the biggest impact, it's clear to see that the concept was sound. Let's take America's meteoric rise in the beer world as an example. It was started by just a few people, in some cases in their living rooms. Humble beginnings but big ambitions. Jim Koch of Boston Brewing Company decided that lager didn't need to be dumbed down to be enjoyable. Ken Grossman of Sierra Nevada discovered the power of American hops and set out to show everyone what they could do. Goose Island's Greg Hall wanted to combine the big-flavoured beer with the American traditions of barrel-aging whisky.

All three of these ideas are brilliant – the kind of ideas that make you wonder how they had never been done before. The kind of idea that leaves you kicking yourself because it wasn't you that came up with it. They had the power to change the course of brewing, and they created three cracking beers that prepped the market for thousands of others to do the same.

With the brewing world blown wide open there are ideas cropping up all over the place. What started as a very American revolution has spread across the globe. That's been fantastic for the quality of beer we can drink, but it's made standing out a lot harder. Now the ideas seem much more subtle, while setting yourself apart has become even more important. It could be dry-hopping at an unusual time to create a new style, adding ingredients no one has thought of using, or reverting back to fermenting in slate and wood like we did centuries ago.

I'm alluding to a lot of famous breweries here, but none of these guys were the first to think of these things. If you want to see future trends in beer, look to the home brewers. They are the guys experimenting in their garages with no commercial or time pressures. They make beer just for themselves, and they can experiment without the worry of wasting huge amounts of ingredients, time or money. There's not a brewery in the world that doesn't have at least one brewer who started at home with a massive pan, a plastic spoon and a head full of dreams.

## HUNDREDS, MAYBE THOUSANDS

Jim, Ken and Greg probably had their ideas at the same time as a thousand others, but these were the guys who managed to convey that great idea in a beer. They took a concept and by chance or design made it look, feel and taste special. The beer in their heads became the beer in the glass, which is a much harder process than your average drinker realises. Even before you get to the art of it, the science is tough enough.

The Brad and I are often asked what makes a great brewery. It took years to find a satisfactory answer and, sadly, it wasn't either of us who first said it. It was Sam McMeekin, the cofounder of Gipsy Hill Brewing Company, who noted that a great brewery does everything 1% better than its nearest rival. I love that idea.

While brewing, there are hundreds, maybe thousands, of touch points where decisions have to be made and actions taken. It could be the mash temperature, the hop regime, the time in barrel or anything else along the brewing timeline. What your decisions are and when you enact them is the difference between a great idea and a great beer. The first touchpoint is the ingredients, and that's where the idea starts to take shape.

# CHAPTER

3

# THE GRAIN

Y ou can make beer without hops, you make beer without cultivated yeast, and you can make beer without water (oh yes). But you can't make it without grain.

Grain was the key to the discovery of beer and, in fact, alcohol. A stone tablet chiseled in Sumeria (now Iraq) shows the world's first hipsters enjoying a beer through straws from a single communal bowl. We think they're using straws because their beer filtration techniques weren't exactly up to scratch, so essentially they were sucking on old porridge.

Historians believe beer was discovered when these people were making bread and left the spent grain or leftover dough out in the rain. A few days later some hungry fellow decided to eat some, and suddenly he found that he could dance better and his self-esteem issues had gone away. I jest, but he would have certainly felt a little light-headed and rather good about himself. It must have been a feeling quite unlike any he had ever experienced – a feeling they put down to a gift from god – so it's no wonder the Sumerians tried to replicate it.

Their grain recipe – or "malt bill" – was very simple: one kind of grain, crushed by hand. It's hard to know which grain it was because any cereal with starch has the ability to be turned into alcohol, but archaeologists have found evidence from the time to suggest it was barley. This grain remains the most important in brewing.

The myriad reasons for this will make you marvel at the wonder of barley. There are two ways in which it is perfect. The first is that it has the best combination of enzymes and starch concentrations, which allows for greater utilisation and extract of sugars. To put that in English, barley has lots of sugars that are easy to turn into alcohol (we'll talk more about that process later).

My favourite reason is that barley has a husk – a tough outer shell that protects it from damage. That makes it easy to handle, but more importantly it means that when you pour water through the crushed grain, it self-filters to allow clear sugary liquid to come through. It's as if barley was born for brewing; it has literally shaped itself to be as helpful as possible for the process.

It would be remiss not to mention the other grains involved in brewing, so props to wheat for your sweet, full body; rye for your tangy bite; and buckwheat for letting coeliacs live a little for once. Oh, and screw you, maize. Stop ruining our lagers.

We'll be making references to all these grains during this chapter, but before we do we need to explain why it's called malt rather than grain because it's fundamental to how beer is made and why it tastes like it does.

# THE MALTING PROCESS

There are two main kinds of barley used for malting – two-row and six-row. This refers to the number of kernels growing adjacent to each other on the ear. Two-row is best because the proteins and starch are more evenly distributed, making it a more predictable grain to malt and brew with. Six-row is just cheaper, so a good brewer wouldn't touch it and neither will we.

Grains like barley are full of starch, a form of energy that yeast can't ferment, so we "malt" it to make it easy for them. First, the

grain is steeped in tepid water to hydrate the starch and activate the enzymes – the perfect state to sprout shoots and grow.

The process of shooting is known as germination. The seeds are left to germinate on giant, humidified warehouse floors. During this time, the tough starches break down into powdery mill that will turn to sugar during the mash. The grain is then kilned to dry it out and stop it growing into full-on barley before we can brew with it.

So far, so flavourless. It's when we get kilning that malt gets exciting. As well as preserving the enzymes and sugar for the mash, maltsters can add colour and flavour in the kiln. The characteristics it picks up during this process play a huge part in defining a beer's style. What follows is a simple breakdown of the malts you'll find in a beer. It's not a comprehensive list – there are books on the stuff – but all the other kinds are simply regional variations on these themes.

The first two are known as base malts – lighter grains that make up the majority of any malt bill. This is because they provide all the sugars and enzymes for the mash, and it only takes a tiny amount of dark malt to totally change a beer.

# PILSNER MALT

Used mostly for – you guessed it – lagers, pilsner malt is the lightest of the malts because it has been kilned at such a low temperature (70-80°C or 160°F) that very little colour is added to the grain. Think of it like being put into stasis – nothing has really changed, and nothing will until water is reintroduced during the mash to get the chemical processes going again.

Pilsner malt is bready, sweet and slightly honey-like when it's really good stuff.

## PALE ALE

Pale malt is the tiniest shade darker, thanks to being kilned a little hotter, and is the base for most modern ales including the famous American IPA. That hotter oven makes it more biscuity, though it remains sweet and pale like pilsner.

## VIENNA

The malt that gives Vienna lager its name, Vienna is the first so-called "coloured" malt. It's not too far off pale ale malt, but it's been roasted quicker at around 110°C (230°F). Usually it's used sparingly to add some toastiness, but when used in larger quantities it makes for a much darker beer – like Brooklyn Lager.

## MUNICH

Munich malt is slightly unusual in that it involves the extra step of "stewing." The grains are slowly cooked in water for around two hours at 40°C (105°F) to make more sugar available. It's then quickly kilned, so the sugar caramelizes. Slightly darker than the base malts, Munich malt forms the bulk of Bocks, Märzens and many lagers where the brewer wants a little more colour and a fuller, malty flavour. Munich is also what gives ESBs their rich mouthfeel and depth. It's not sweeter, but it's somehow richer.

# CRYSTAL

Crystal malt is made in the same way as Munich but at 60°C (140°F) with the malt in full-on starch-to-sugar conversion. It's then kilned at a higher temperature to imbue the malt with a sweet, toffee-like flavour. It's commonly used in American IPAs to balance out all the hop bitterness.

# ACIDULATED MALT

Another strange one, acidulated malt is used to help turn a beer sour or lower the pH of a beer (we'll explain why you'd want that soon). It's made in the same way as all the other malts, except that it is either sprayed or naturally coated with lactic acid to lower its pH and taste more tart.

# AMBER

You're going to feel silly for even reading this one, but amber malt is a more toasted version of the pale ale that is used to give beers an amber hue and notes of slightly burnt toast and caramel.

# BROWN

Now we're getting into the dark malts. Brown malts are roasted to the colour of tree bark, to add a nuttiness and earthiness to beer while retaining a slight caramel note. Brown malts are used to add depth to porters, and, obviously, in brown ales.

# SMOKED (RAUCHMALZ)

Smoked malts were made famous by the truly amazing Schlenkerla brewpub in Bamberg, Germany. Instead of kilning, producers of Rauchmalz smoke the grains over an open flame until they are dark and toasted. The best way to describe the resulting aroma is like bacon being cooked over a campfire.

# CHOCOLATE

No need to tell you what colour or flavour this imparts in a beer, except to add that it can also imbue a complex coffee aroma, too. It's not sweet at all because we reach the point of literally burning the sugar. In fact, it can add to the perceived bitterness of a beer, so you have to hop carefully after using this malt.

# BLACK

Well the maltster just went and burnt it, didn't he? I like to think this was invented when the guy in charge of the furnace got distracted (or went off for a beer). Anyway, black malt is roasted to the point of carbonising, so it adds an ashy, burnt coffee edge to the beer. It's only ever used in tiny quantities to dry out the finish of a beer and create that sexy black colour.

# THE OTHER GRAINS

Barley isn't the only grain used in beer, and some others are malted, too. Here are the other common brewing grains and how they are used.

## WHEAT

Easily the most common after barley, wheat is used to give beers more body and a subtle sweetness. You can tell it's there by its lighter aroma and signature haze. It's so obvious in beer that it has come to define most of the ones it is used in, such as Wits, Weissbiers and Berlinerweisses. It's also often used in East Coast IPAs and low ABV hoppy beers to give them more body.

## RYE

Imagine eating a slice of rye bread. That's what this grain does to beer on a much more subtle level. It can also add a savoury, earthy twang to it (or a fiery spiciness if you used it with crystal rye), which makes it a devilishly difficult grain to balance out. But Rye IPAs can be fantastic things in the hands of a good brewer.

## OATS

Use of this hearty grain all but died out in brewing until a few years ago when the oatmeal stout made a comeback. Flavour-wise it's hard to detect, but it can make for an exceptionally smooth mouthfeel.

# HOW TO CONSTRUCT A MALT BILL

So we know the science part of the malt, but the art is in balancing all the varying, and often conflicting, characteristics. On top of that, you'll have the drinker's expectations that come from whatever style you decide to write on the label.

The first thing a brewer decides (after the style, of course) is what strength he wants the beer. This correlates to how much base malt you put in compared to how much water. There are lots of other factors, but that is the basic sum: more malt equals more booze. Sometimes when a brewer makes a really strong beer, they have to use all kinds of tricks to fit the malt in the mash tun (once I saw a brewer prop his sparge arm up with bricks to stop it skimming the mash).

The visuals come next. People drink first with their eyes (not literally, that would be agony), so you need it to look delicious. If it's a stout, then you want it black as the night. If it's an IPA, then you want it to glow amber like a golden chalice. Brewers have to think about mouthfeel, too. Lagers need to be light and zingy, so they can jump off the palate, while a weissbier needs to feel like velvet from the moment it hits your lips.

All the while, you need to focus on the most important thing: the flavour. It's what we're all here for, and your intention has to be spot on. If I'm drinking a black IPA, I want to taste the toast and liquorice as well as the grapefruit and resin. If it's an American red, then I want crystal sweetness, but it should never be cloying.

Making a malt bill is a balancing act. It's a part of the recipe a brewer rarely gets right first time because coming at the start of the process means everything you do afterwards will have an impact. And at no point is that more clear than during the mash.

# CHAPTER

# THE MASH

**B**y the time you head to work in the morning, the chances are every brewer in the country has mashed in and is wondering where his next cup of tea is coming from.

Brewdays can take anything from five to twelve hours, and then there's a lot of cleaning up to do, so it starts absurdly early. Brewing collaboration beers or filming on location usually means we get the first train of the day, but it's always worth it. The steamy aroma of a mash is, without doubt, my favourite smell in the world. It's somewhere between a great cask bitter and a cookie fresh from the oven. However long you've been a brewer, especially on winter days, you can't help but lean over the tun and breathe in the delicious, warming steam.

Mashing is the process of extracting flavour and sugar from the malt and introducing water to the beer. Hot water and malt are added to a mash tun – a giant vat with a filter plate at the bottom of it. There, it's held at the best temperatures for enzymes to break down the starch into sugar, stirred most of the time by hand or machine.

The mash may sound like a giant porridge, but it's where a huge part of a beer's character comes from. It's not just affecting the flavour, aroma and colour that we talked about in the last chapter, either – it controls the mouthfeel of the beer, too, and nailing that is very tricky indeed.

# THE GOLDILOCKS THEORY

If Goldilocks had broken into the bears' house when they were homebrewing, she would have really had her work cut out. Mostly we talk about temperature when mashing, but there are a lot more variables at play. There's sugar, enzymes and pH levels for her to judge too. The science of the mash is balancing them to get the perfect malty liquid – or "wort" – for the style of beer you're making.

It's worth noting here that no recipe is ever really "finished" – good brewers are always tweaking their processes to refine perceived flaws or to react to a shift in an ingredient. So there's no right or wrong way to do a particular mash; there are only principles that every brewer interprets in their own way. This variation between styles and ingredients, brewers and breweries, is part of what makes beer so varied and exciting. But it also makes writing about beer almost as hard as brewing it. So cheers, guys.

## THE RIGHT AMOUNT OF WATER

The next chapter deals with the kind of water we need to use, but the amount of water in the mash is also key. Enzymes are pretty excitable, so if you don't water down the grain enough they will go to town on the starch and covert it to sugar rapidly. The problem with that is they might do a half-assed job, and some of the sugar they create won't be fermentable. The result is a fuller-bodied, sweeter beer. A mash with lots of water will result in a slower conversion, but more fermentable sugar for a drier beer. Neither situation is necessarily better; they are just suited to different styles of beer and brewing. A drier mash,

particularly one with higher protein grains like wheat, does run the risk of getting "stuck."

# THE RIGHT TEMPERATURE

Now here comes the science bit. These enzymes I've mentioned only work at certain temperatures, and, inconveniently, they all work at different ones.

We could get bogged down in glucanase and peptidases – all the "ases" – but all we need to know is that these two help keep the beer clear and improve retention of the foamy head. More important to us are the alpha and beta amylases that break down the starch. Think of the alpha as a maniac lumberjack with a chainsaw who is chopping down trees at random, while the beta is a madman with an axe splintering smaller pieces off the trees. The yeast can only consume the small bits, so alpha doesn't give them much to work with because it chops all kinds of sizes. Beta, meanwhile, chops at the bases and makes lots of little fermentable bits. Beta turns most of the starch to sugar, but it can only reach so high, so a little bit gets missed.

The reason I'm over-investing in this metaphor is because this is where the mouthfeel and lots of the flavour is decided. Because the alpha enzymes like chainsawing at high temperatures (around 70°C/158°C) and the betas want to start chopping at cooler ones (around 62°C/144°F), the temperature you mash at is vital to the rest of the brew.

If you mash at the lower ranges of the beta zone, you'll end up with a thinner, drier beer. That's because the betas broke down most of the thick body-providing starch chains, turning them into sugar that was eaten up by the yeast.

If you mash at a higher temperature, you'll get fuller-bodied, sweeter beer because the alphas didn't break down all the chunky chains of starch into sugar, leaving it unfermentable.

Most beers are mashed right in between these two ranges. It gives you the sugar you need while not taking away all the body from the beer. When writing a recipe, this is taken as the standard that the brewer deviates from to tailor his mash to the beer in his head. It may be he is making a big imperial IPA and needs all the sugar he can get, so he'll mash in low. Conversely, if he's making a 3.8% session IPA, he'll mash high to leave some body and unfermented sweetness to inject flavour.

As the temperature ranges are pretty small, accuracy is key – keeping control of the mash temperature, and nailing it at the start (known as the "strike temperature"), is vital to get it like Goldilocks wanted: just right.

# THE RIGHT ACIDITY

The enzymes at work in the mash prefer a specific pH, so most brewers aim at between 5.2 and 5.5. That's pretty much the Golden Rule unless you're making a sour beer, and even then the drop in pH usually happens during fermentation even when you're using acidulated malt.

Getting the pH of the mash right is a bit of a battle because the kind of malt you add changes it. Thankfully, most water supplies are slightly alkali and, if you're lucky, nature can do the work for you because dark malts lower the pH. You can also tweak the mash using brewing salts, but this can have an effect on the flavour of the beer. German brewers—who have to stick to certain rules to adhere to that all-important marketing tool, the Reinheitsgebot—use a little acidulated malt to get the right pH.

# THE RIGHT TIME

You can mash for as long as you want. Usually it's for around an hour, but for an imperial stout it could be several to convert all the starch. The longer you do it, the more sugar you will extract because the enzymes will have more time to work. A longer mash also allows brewers time to change the temperature of the mash – going through the beta temperatures up to the alpha to break down as much as possible. However, not all mash tuns are set up for this, so most brewers stick to one temperature.

# THE RIGHT GRAVITY

Brewing is all about having a clear destination in mind, and in the mash that destination is the correct "original gravity." This is a measurement of the sugar-to-water ratio in the sugary liquid that is now known as "wort". Too high and the beer could be more alcoholic than intended, too low and it could be weaker. At the end of fermentation, the "final gravity" – or remaining sugar concentration – is measured and the difference between the two reveals the ABV (alcohol by volume) of the beer.

In homebrewing, the gravity is measured using a hydrometer, which is a long, absurdly thin glass tube that floats in the wort. The original gravity is indicated by how high it sits in the liquid. Ask any homebrewer how many times they have smashed their hydrometer and you will learn what most of them think of this particular piece of equipment. Only a little more robust is the refractometer, which is less accurate but has the advantage of making the brewer look like a pirate.

Getting the right gravity is a tricky little game played by brewers once the mash is over. The malt has been steeped, stirred and broken down to release its sugar, so now the brewer needs to collect it. This is done by opening up the bottom of the mash tun and pouring hot water (around 168°F) in from the top. This water filters through the grain, collecting all the sugar before making its way into the next vessel, the kettle. This process is known as "sparging" or, when using a second vessel called a lauter tun, "lautering."

As it goes through, the brewer takes a sample to measure. From that, he works out how much water he'll need to get the right original gravity. This happens several times during the so-called "run off" because the first few litres of wort are usually more concentrated than the last few. Lovely as water is, the last thing he wants to do is add too much and end up diluting the beer.

# CHAPTER

# THE WATER

B eer is 90% water – nearly 100% if it's a crap macrolager – but this vital ingredient is often overlooked. As an amateur and highly impatient homebrewer, I'd rather spend my time sniffing hops than playing with water chemistry, but that's my loss. The closest brewers have come to mastering nature is through the water they use.

Water chemistry is actually much more exciting than it sounds. It's been hugely influential on the history of beer thanks to the fact that we haven't always had such control over it. Different kinds of water are best suited to different styles and where each kind of water appeared, so did a certain type of beer. Brewers have long been able to make small adjustments to their water, but these days they can design it to exact specifications.

NOTE: Once water has been heated up in a brewery, it is no longer known as water. It becomes liquor, so don't be surprised to see that term used in this book…or any other beer book, for that matter.

# WHAT KIND OF WATER IS BEST?

Let's be straight from the start. Tasty beer can be brewed from all kinds of water, so don't let any brewer tell you theirs is the best in the world, or that theirs lends any magical property to the beer. Unless it's Vaclav, Head Brewer at Pilsner Urquell, because he is not a man to be argued with and his water is delicious.

That said, water chemistry can be the difference between a good beer and a great beer. There are two variables the brewer needs to be aware of with his water supply. One is the pH and the other in the mineral content. pH can be perfected in many ways, from diluting with water from a different source to using salts and specific grains in the mash. The more exciting side is the minerals because brewers can use these to "season" the beer.

At its most basic, brewers want moderately hard water. The hardness of the water refers to the concentration of calcium and magnesium, which are important in the brewing process. They are nutrients for the yeast and play other roles in the stability of the beer. Too much will affect the flavour, however, leading to a nasty tannic (powdery) quality.

Outside of calcium and magnesium, there are a few more minerals that are vital to a beer's profile. As with everything in brewing, striking the balance is key so you don't get spiky off-flavours. Sodium contributes to the body and maltiness of a beer, but the beer can be salty if too much is used. Chloride does a similar job, but it can add a chemical aroma and flavour. Sulfate is an interesting one because it can enhance perceived hop bitterness, something played with by brewers of less hoppy styles to get a cleaner finish.

The use of sulfate is a great example of how the ideal water chemistry changes depending on the style of beer being made. That's where the mysticism comes from with brewing water. Even today, water from certain parts of the world is looked to and recreated to get the signature flavours of that region.

DUBLIN

BURTON UPON TRENT

LONDON

PILSEN

# EUROPE'S FAMOUS BREWING WATERS

In some cases, the water has become as famous as the beers they've helped create.

## PILSEN, CZECH REPUBLIC

The water in Pilsen is exceptionally soft and low in minerals. That's one of the main reasons that the lagers produced there are unique. The lack of astringency makes for a very smooth beer, and the low sulfates means they can pile in much more of the aromatic saaz hop before the bitterness becomes too much. The result is a rounded, sweet and hoppy beer like Pilsner Urquell. That particular brewery loves the local water so much that it brings it to the brewery from a well several kilometres away, and they're not the only ones who source from a specific well. To serve beers at Oktoberfest, a brewery must pull its water from the well within the Munich walls. Only six brewers currently can, and they won't be changing their source any time soon.

## LONDON, ENGLAND

London brewing is most famous for one style – porter. Supposedly drunk by the port workers on the docks, this beer is rich, roasty and coffee-like with little in the way of hop aroma. This suits the uniquely hard water that London brewers were forced to work with. Such mineral-rich water could easily create unwanted flavours in the beer and create a mash too alkali for the yeast. Using roasted malt brings down the pH, and being sparing with the hops still resulted in a bitter finish thanks to the mineral content.

## BURTON ON TRENT, ENGLAND

If God intended us to brew beer, then he intended us to brew it in Burton. The water there is so perfect for the most popular craft beer style that it is almost beyond coincidence. Burton is the spiritual home of IPA, and was once the brewing capital of the world, all thanks to its mineral-rich water. It's high in sulphate, which gives it a clean and assertive bitterness, and it is low in sodium, which might cause distracting maltiness or minerality.

## DUBLIN, IRELAND

Dublin is famous for one thing in beer – Guinness. And it's no accident that the beer is as dark and roasty as beer gets. The water in Dublin is exceptionally alkaline, which means getting the ideal pH of 5.2-5.5 would have been almost impossible 100 years ago without lots of dark, acidic malt. On top of that, it's pretty low in all the bitterness-enhancing minerals. Hence why Guinness is, for all its other flaws, a wonderfully balanced beer.

So as you may have gathered, delicious soft water is perfect for lighter, subtler beers. But for the big styles you need minerals to back it up, and those beer styles were traditionally brewed wherever that kind of water is to be found. Nowadays brewing water may be more chemistry than anything, but it has been an instrumental part of beer's millennia-long journey to where it is today. Next we're going to talk about an ingredient that is a more recent development than you might think.

# CHAPTER

# THE HOPS

I f you thought you liked hops then you're going to be utterly in love by the end of this chapter. Full disclosure: I am a complete hophead, a lupulin monster, an alpha acid obsessive. At my funeral I want a wreath of citra on my coffin.

And that would be less insane than it sounds because hops are just flowers. Found on long vines that grow in temperate soils all around the world, they aren't the best-looking flowers, but they are certainly the best smelling. You see, hops are responsible for nearly all the citrusy, edgy aromas in beer. If it's fruity and has a piney twang to it then you can bet humulus lupulus is behind it.

These incredible flowers – or cones, as they are called in the biz – smell like they do because of the essential oils they contain. All plant matter contains essential oils to some degree. Many share the same ones, which is why hops smell similar to unlikely things like cannabis (actually a distant relative of hops).

These essential oils are also known as "volatile oils" because they have a tendency to break apart. That very act of breaking apart is why we can smell them so clearly even in small quantities, but it also makes them very delicate. Brewers have to handle them with care during brewing. They also have to store them in cold rooms to keep them as fresh as possible, because fresh hops mean more aroma.

Another important part of the hop is the resin, which contains the acids that make beer bitter. We'll get on to that in the next chapter, but some hops are more bitter than others, and this has to be taken into account when making a recipe.

The amount of acids and oils in a hop varies hugely. It's handy here to think of hops like grapes in wine – you have the variety of hop and then the place where it's grown. The characteristics of a hop variety come down to its lineage. Most hops in the world are hybrid versions of other more established varieties. The big citrus hops from the West Coast that kick-started the craft beer revolution may seem extreme, but they are all offshoots of subtler British, German and Czech hops that have been bred to yield certain qualities – in most cases a metric ton of fruity aroma. There are farms all over the world interbreeding hops in the hope of creating super-varieties that add as much aroma and flavour as possible, but impart the least bitterness and are the most resistant to disease.

But the where and when of hops matters too. There's lots of evidence to show that flavour, aroma and bitterness can vary between fields and even vines, so the heritage of a hop is getting more important as we come to understand the plant better. Nowadays, hops largely come from five parts of the world and each has its own sub-regions. They all bring something special to the world of hoppy beer thanks to the local varieties, soils and climates. West Coast hops are famous for their big citrus and pine aromas; Antipodean hops for tropical vibes and white-wine-like acidity; British hops for their spicy, earthy savouriness; German hops for their lemon crispness; and Czech hops for a grassy, subtle citric edge. These are, of course, huge generalisations. So let's get a bit more specific.

# TOP OF THE HOPS

These are, to our mind, the most important hops in the world. It could be because of their aroma and flavour, the beers they are used in, or their place in the hop family tree, but we think these are the guys that have made beer what it is today – and will make it what it is tomorrow.

## SAAZ

One of the "noble" European hops. Lots of varieties have sprung from this Czech legend. It's the hop that gives Bohemian lagers their zing, with lots of grassy, lemony crispness and some almost strawberry-like fruitier notes in big doses.

## BRAMLING CROSS

Sadly dismissed as a dull British varietal, Bramling Cross is a subtle beast, but it can load a beer with richer, almost blackcurrant and lemon-like, notes. That makes it great in roasty beers and for adding aromatic depth to lighter, citrusy beers.

## FUGGLES

Fuggles is widely maligned for being flavourless, but back in 1949 it accounted for 78% of all English hops. A bunch of West Coast, dank IPA lovers just passed out at the thought, but back then Fuggles gave more than enough spice and bitterness to satisfy drinkers. It balanced the malt and not much more, which is exactly what it was asked to do.

# GOLDINGS

A catch-all for a huge variety of European hops, this variety takes its name from where it is grown – East Kent Goldings, for example. It's been hugely important in ales for centuries as well as the father plant to all kinds of charismatic hops.

# HALLETAU

Another noble hop, Halletau is the father of many massive aromatic hops. On its own it is famous for a spicy and lemony character with very low bitterness, making it ideal for the lighter helles lagers of southern Germany. Hard as it is to explain the aroma, you know when a lager has been hopped with it.

# CASCADE

The hop that changed everything. Invented during the hunt for mildew-resistant hops, Cascade is a combination of Fuggles, Russian Serebrianke and an mystery hop – a fairly plain upbringing with remarkable results. It was the start of grapefruit, pine, citrus and even notes of blueberry in beer. It was made famous by the still-delicious Sierra Nevada Pale Ale, one of the best West Coast beers ever made.

# CITRA

I could write sonnets about Citra and its huge grapefruit notes, subtle pithiness and pine, hint of juicy fruitiness and slightly savoury, heady edge. If ever there was a hop to sum up hops, it would be this one. Hence why it is one of the most sought-after and expensive varieties in the world.

# AMARILLO

We've included Amarillo in this list over lots of awesome "c" hops—like Centennial and Columbus—because its citrusy aroma is uniquely orangey. It can be like sniffing orange peel or biting into a Satsuma. You can use it in stouts for a chocolate orange vibe, or in IPAs for a mega pithy citrus edge, or in a pale ale for its implied juicy sweetness.

# SIMCOE

Dank and delicious, this hop is much loved on the West coast. It can bring lots of citrus to the party, but it brings even more earthy pine and resin. When really fresh it can be almost onion-like or borderline weed-like. Some people love that and other people hate it. The Brad and I are on either side of that line.

# MOSAIC

My personal favourite hop, Mosaic, can be summed up in one brand name – Juicy Fruit. It's just silly fruity with lots of passion fruit and lychee while also having an almost liquorice-like sting. Used right, it just leaps out of the glass.

# EL DORADO

Big aroma hops tend to grow in the cooler climates of the world, hence why most of the famous US hops are grown in the Yakima Valley in Washington State, near Seattle. The king of them all is El Dorado because of its massive tropical aroma. This hop takes that tutti frutti, overripe mango vibe to the extreme and is now hugely popular in the new, less bitter East Coast IPAs.

## SORACHI ACE

A bizarre and brilliant hop, Sorachi Ace is a bit like a funhouse mirror – whichever way you use it you'll end up with something totally different. We've got the following aromas from this hop on different occasions – coconut, strawberry, vanilla, armpit, leather. Go figure.

## NELSON SAUVIN

Named after the grape that it imitates, this tropical-tinged hop also has a hint of acidity in the form of gooseberry and a delicate white-wine-like lingering note, too. It's truly unique, outrageously fruity and smooth.

Of course, the thing to remember is that hops are present in nearly all beers – even the macro-ist of macro beers use them, and they likely use very nice hops indeed. It's what you do with the hops that counts. Give a bad chef the best ingredients in the world and he'll still overcook the beef, butcher the vegetables and burn the sauce. Give free rein to an expert and he will make something greater than the sum of its parts. The remaining brewing chapters are about how a brewer can make the most of hops; how they can perform the magic that makes an alcoholic beverage naturally smell like mango juice, or coconut, or whatever it is in the brewer's head. Much as I love hops, I love brewers more.

# THE HOP HARVEST

The man's cigarette is almost finished. It's crept up towards his lips so slowly that he hasn't noticed, and the ash is curling towards the ground, pattering to his feet as he speaks.

The man is talking in Czech at high speed about his hops, acres and acres of which span into the distance behind him. He only pauses for breath so our translator can get a word in to explain what he is saying. He's young, brash and not in the least like the labourers toiling behind him, pulling at vines and loading tractors with hops. He explains that, despite the arduous work, it is the best time of the year for him and his community. It is a guaranteed work for labourers, but it's more than that. They are at the start of the process of making beer, and in the Czech Republic there is little more important than that.

We meander in and out of the Saaz vines. You can't help but smile at the scale of them. Sometimes we wonder how so small a flower can add so much aroma to a beer, but when they are like this it makes more sense. Five times the height of the tallest man and bushy with flowers, these vines feel like soldiers lined up for battle. And they are heroes in the Czech Republic. That night we head into Pilsen for the annual Hop Harvest festival. Brewers and food stands lined the streets, and the whole town turned out for live music in the square. Vines are entwined around lampposts and fences. People wear crowns of hops and toast to the season.

For The Brad and me, it is one of the defining moments of our beer adventures – to see a whole nation as in love with beer as we are.

# CHAPTER

S o we know what hops are and what they can add to the beer, but how do they do it? Well, if we made porridge during the mash, now we're making tea.

The run-off from the mash is transported to the "kettle" (this metaphor is awesome!) where the water is brought to boiling point and held there for anything between 60 minutes and several hours. The hops are added at various points during this time to achieve different effects. There's a lot of debate (or rather slightly drunken philosophising) about the whats and whens of hop additions, but one key rule will always remain true: the earlier you add a hop, the more bitterness it will impart. Think of it like overstewed tea. The longer it is in there, the more astringency goes into the water.

The opposite is true of aroma. If you add lots of amazing, aromatic hops to the start of the boil, then those essential oils will break down and the aromas and flavours boil off. This has led to two terms being used by brewers to differentiate the two roles of the hops – the early "bittering addition" and the late "aroma addition." As you're about to find out, people's palates have shifted towards fruitier aromas, causing the emphasis on hopping to move backwards toward the aroma additions.

In single hop beers the brewer will use one variety of hop for both bittering and aroma, but in most brews they are different. Some hops, like Pilgrim, Magnum and Willamette, are mostly used as bittering hops because they contain the right levels of certain acids that add a clean, non-astringent bitterness to the beer when boiled for a long time.

So it's not just time that affects the bitterness. It's the level of alpha acids in the hops, too. These acids are soluble, so they permeate the wort and spread bitterness. For beer, this is exactly what we want to balance the sweet malts, but the brewer has to be careful. He must use the acid level of his hops to calculate exactly how many hops he wants to use and how long he will boil them for. This calculation results in the International Bittering Unit (IBU), which is the official measurement of a beer's bitterness (see panel).

Big aromatic hops are wasted when used at the start of the boil because all the flavour and aroma is broken down. Instead, they are usually added a few minutes before, or slightly after, the end of the boil. These hops impart almost no bitterness because alpha acids only break down at temperatures around 79°C/175°F. Instead, the essential oils become soluble and enter the wort, filling it with delicate flavour that it is now the job of the brewer to protect.

To give you an idea of how some classic beers are made, we've provided a graph with the rough timings for bittering and aroma additions so you get an idea of how hops are distributed throughout the boil.

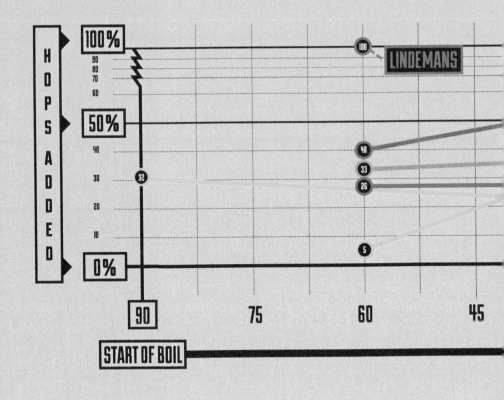

## BREWDOG PUNK IPA

Punk uses lots of hops at the start and the finish to give a bold bitterness and aroma. They also load the kettle with Nelson Sauvin to up the acidity and tropical fruit.

## BROOKLYN LAGER

Brooklyn use a fairly modest amount of hops because their lager is about the malts, and you'll see it's spread evenly throughout the boil for plenty of flavour and bitterness without the citrus aroma dominating.

## FULLERS LONDON PORTER

Again, it's fairly front-loaded, but the use of some English hops brings lightness and acidity to the beer when fresh. Notice that there are no hops at the end of the boil so the main aroma from the beer can come from the malts.

## GIPSY HILL DRIFTER

We brewed this beer with our friends at Gipsy Hill in tribute to the amazing ultra fruity IPAs of the East Coast. It's almost all added after the

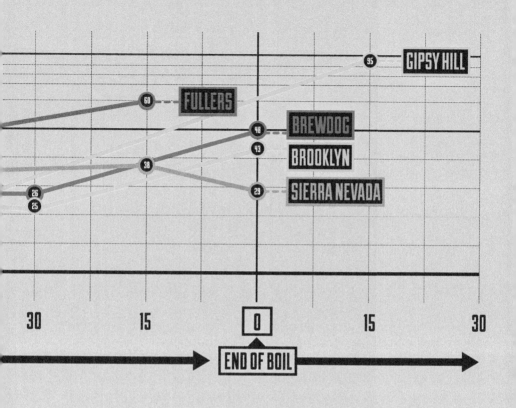

GIPSY HILL 95

FULLERS 60

BREWDOG 48

BROOKLYN 43

SIERRA NEVADA 29

38

26
25

30    15    0    15    30

END OF BOIL

boil has simmered down to make for a huge tropical aroma and as little bitterness as possible.

## SIERRA NEVADA PALE ALE

This world-famous beer makes great use of the cascade hop, and was one of the first in the world to do so. That said, we were surprised by how the hops were spread out throughout the boil, which make it a more traditional recipe than we expected. However, the quantities involved mean this is still a deliciously hoppy beer.

## LINDEMANS OUDE GUEUZE

Belgian lambics use a fair amount of hops, but they age them to remove bitterness and flavour. The hops here simply protect the beer from unwanted infection during its years in barrels.

# NEW TRADITIONS

Through the craft beer world's obsession with IPAs, hops have almost come to define the entire movement. I've heard traditionalists complain about modern styles lacking complexity, over-aweing palates and smelling synthetic – one memorable term was "hipster disco juice" – but these complaints miss the point. True, we all love a "session beer" that we can knock back over a long evening with friends. But every now and then we want a beer to blow us sideways with its aroma, to get all up in our headspace and scream "hey, look at me! I've been hopped so late the brewer didn't get to kiss his kids goodnight!"

This late hopping is a relatively new style of brewing, and once our obsession fades from Exorcist-like possession back down to mild hysteria, it will sit happily next to all the other beer styles we once considered extreme. You never hear traditionalists complain a Belgian kriek is too cherry-like, or a weissbier too banana-y, because any brewer will tell you that hops aren't the only way to inject huge fruity flavours into beer. Malt can bring lots of darker fruits to the party, but combining hop flavours and aromas with the yeast is where beer can be its most complex and exciting.

# THE BITTER ARMS RACE

Back in the days of the British Empire, hops were used in beer purely for their antiseptic qualities. They could stop a beer getting infected, and they would help to balance the slight sourness that all beer had thanks to the wilder yeast strains in brewing at the time.

The famous India Pale Ale, so called because it was sent over to expats in India when it was a British colony, was a damned hoppy beer for its day. Brewed in Burton with its mineral-rich water and then hopped with British varieties from Kent to survive months at sea, it was the bitterest beer so far. But it had nothing on the IPAs we know now, at least not once it had sat in a barrel and mellowed on the way to India.

The first craft beers that started coming out of American beer geeks' garages in the late 1970s were significantly more bitter thanks to the use of new hybrid American hops like cascade. Far from balancing the malts, these beers focused on the hop aroma at the expense of all other flavours. They carried more alpha acids and were used in greater quantities. As a result, these beers were invariably more challenging than their ancestors and macro rivals. It took patience and serious evangelism for this style to gain traction but, slowly, it is going mainstream in the US and UK.

The reasons for this go beyond the amazing aromas and flavours. Contrary to what some believe, it's no new, hip trend. You see, the funny thing about bitterness is that it is slightly addictive. Bitterness is always the last thing we taste when we eat or drink something because it is the flavour that warns your brain of poison. So when we drink a hugely hoppy IPA for the first time, a little alarm goes off in our brains saying: "YOU JUST DRANK SOMETHING DANGEROUS." When we don't keel over and die, some taste therapists (that's a thing, apparently) say we get a little hit of adrenaline – much like when we go on a roller coaster and scare the living hell out of ourselves. For some, adrenaline is addictive, so once they have one hit they have to have another, and a bigger one each time. Much like spice, we try it and enjoy it, but we slowly build a resistance to it. So we have to have more and more to get that same effect.

This process caused craft brewers, particularly in the States, to enter into a subconscious bitter arms race, trying to make the bitterest, biggest IPA they could. It culminated in beers up in the 1000 IBUs that were, to most palates, undrinkable.

It also resulted in the phenomenon that Vince Cilurzo, founder of the world-famous Russian River Brewing Company, called the Lupulin Threshold Shift. This is not a weapon on the Starship Enterprise, but rather the idea that a once brilliant, exciting hoppy beer can be deemed tame in a matter of months as brewers continue their mission of one-upmanship to make bolder IPAs.

The thing is, bitterer isn't always better. It can make a beer chewy or medicinal, and it can even distract from the fruitiness. Great beers that have stood the test of time, like Vince's Pliny the Elder, are not 120-IBU monsters. They are more balanced and nuanced. Thankfully, there has been an even greater shift towards late hopping – more in the fermenter than the kettle – at the expense of bitterness. We're all for that, as the lack of bitter tolerance is the biggest barrier to new drinkers getting into good beer.

# CHAPTER

# THE YEAST

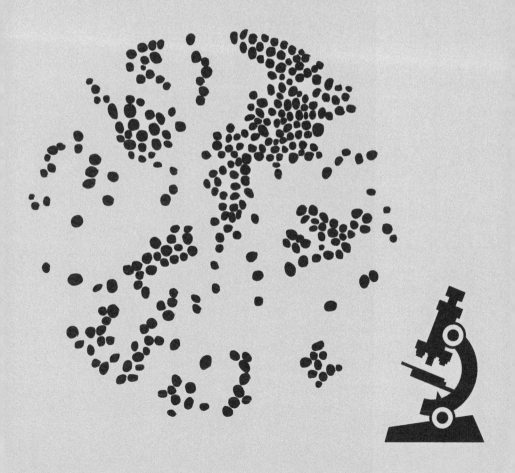

In the days before my obsession with beer, I genuinely thought that there was only one kind of yeast. One uber yeast responsible for beer, wine, bread, Marmite, and thrush.*

In fact, yeast is all around us. It's in your beer and bread, sure. But it's also in the trees, on that table, in that man's beard and even in the air we're breathing. This wild yeast is broadly the same as the one we put into our beers (in some cases exactly the same). It was these strains that were responsible for the world's first-ever beer at least 6,000 years ago.

Nowadays, most brewers use cultivated yeasts that are harvested and then controlled and bred to produce certain characteristics. We haven't made them all the same, though, because that would make all beers taste too similar.

You see, I have come to realise that yeast is the most underrated ingredient in beer by quite some margin. Yeast strains define a beer's style just as much as the malt bill or hop regime. In every conversation I have had with a brewer about a brew that went wrong, it has always come down to the yeast. Equally, when I research a beer to discover its secrets (and there is at least one behind every great beer), reading about its yeast or fermentation is usually the first port of call. If we are coming to the end of the hop arms race, then the next advancement will be in what yeasts we use and how we use them.

People don't tend to think of yeast as an ingredient because they don't think it adds any flavour. This couldn't be further from the truth. When yeast starts eating the sugar in the fermenter, all kinds of hell breaks lose. Bubbles reach for the sky, fumes become toxic, and pressure builds as it gives off three key biproducts – alcohol, carbon dioxide and esters.

*My girlfriend told me not to write this last one, but I am my own man.

The roles of the first two are obvious: alcohol adds booze and carbon dioxide adds bubbles (if in a sealed container). Esters might be new to you, though. In effect, they are chemical compounds that can smell of all sorts of wonderful things or a variety of terrible things. In countries such as Belgium, esters, not hop aromas, are the heroes. Why does your gueuze taste like cider? Yeast. Why does your saison smell a bit like green apple? Yeast. But it's not just the Belgians. Why does your German wheat beer smell like banana? Yeast. Why does your English bitter have a hint of stone fruits? Yeast. You get the idea.

Of course, not all esters are desirable. It might be wrong for the style – no one wants a bubblegum lager – or it might just smell plain wrong. But once we think of yeast as a vital flavour source, the places we can take beer become much more varied and exciting. You could use the same water, malts and hops and end up with a totally different beer by using a different yeast.

The easiest way to explain how this amazing little microbe works is to think of it the same way we think of people. Everybody is different and good at different tasks – Brad hasn't written this book because if he did it would be full of wrestling analogies and typos. Likewise, I haven't illustrated it because then it would be full of penis doodles and stick men. The same is true of yeasts – some ferment superfast and leave a bit of a mess, others take longer but leave very little aroma or flavour behind. A few take forever and leave the beer in delicious ruins.

Where a yeast falls on that spectrum is a mix of nature and nurture. A yeast has its favourite way to work, but stressing it out or letting it relax will have different effects. Like the human population, there are only a few different races but endless variety and excitement within them.

There are two main kinds of yeast. The first is sacchronomyces cerevisiae, or "ale yeast," which ferments at the top of a fermenter (so it floats) and is most comfortable working at a nice room temperature. The other type is "lager yeast," saccharomyces pastorianus, which ferments at the bottom of the fermenter and prefers to be kept chilled while working. So there you have it: the only difference between a lager and an ale is the yeast, and anyone who thinks lagers are boring is being dismissive to say the least. Lager is not boring, Bud Light is.

Ale yeast is mostly associated with estery beers – you get more flavours and aromas from fermentation, which you balance against the other ingredients. After resting, lager yeasts produce clean beers that let the other ingredients shine. There are lots of yeasts that fall in between or sit on either side of these two opposites – you can stress out a lager yeast and end up with a lovely fruity beer called a steam beer (think Anchor Brewing Company), or you can really control fermentation of an ale to end up with very hop-forward IPA with little yeasty twang.

Throwing a spanner in the works is a third common type of yeast: the monsterous brettanomyces. This yeast is usually associated with the barrels of Belgian lambic beers, and it is famous for being able to eat lots of sugars that normal ale and lager yeasts can't. This results in a much drier beer, but in doing so adds lots of unique esters that are sometimes compared to cider, sherbet, farmyards and (inexplicably) horse blankets. If you've ever wondered what makes Orval so dry, pithy and zingy, that's the brett that's added to every bottle.

Those are the basic strains of yeast, but delving into them is the exciting part. Just as people grow up, so does yeast. Many brewers have a house yeast strain that they use over and over in their beers. There are breweries that have yeast strains going back centuries, lovingly cared for because of their flavour and capabilities. The yeast at traditional saison brewery Brasserie Dupont in Belgium and Pilsner Urquell's H yeast are about as famous as yeast can get, forming a huge part of what makes the beers and the brands so unique.

Some, particularly Belgium-influenced brewers, have countless strains they use or blend across their beer range. Others will get in special yeasts for certain brews. But they will have all come from or been mixed with another yeast strain, likely procured from another brewery somehow or bought from a yeast bank (yep, that's a thing).

Without food, yeast is dormant, but every time a yeast strain is added to wort it springs to life. Like a glutton it eats all that sugar and then runs out of food, at which point it goes back to sleep – kind of like a food coma. This is called a generation, and with every generation the yeast will mutate thanks to what happened to it during its lifetime. When a brewer harvests the yeast from a previous brew and brings it back to life in a new one, it rises from the ashes like a beer-covered phoenix. But it might act different to the generation before.

This breeding process is really exciting. It's where a brewer can make his mark on the ingredients he uses. This is where the nurture comes into it – the styles a yeast strain is used for, the places it's used in and, most vitally, the temperature it's used at. But we'll get on to that in the next chapter.

This makes fermentation not only the most important part of the brewing process for individual beers, but also for beers hundreds of generations down the line.

# OTHER MICROBES

Yeast isn't the only microbe in action in beer. If a brewer isn't careful (and sometimes even if he is), his beer could get infected with wild bacteria that hang about in the air and on surfaces. These bacteria aren't harmful, but they can totally change a beer's character. Lactobacillus, for example, will lower the pH of the beer to give it a sour, lemony tang, while peadiococcus can give the beer the consistency of gazpacho soup.

Both those things may sound pretty uninviting, but some breweries actively look for these invasions and have produced world-class beers with them. Using lactobacillus is the main way to make a sour beer, and it can be added manually by the brewer or through natural inoculation. The coming together of bacteria and brett yeast can lead to some of the most complex, deeply flavoured beers in the world – the ones made famous by the lambic breweries of the Pajottenland near Brussels, in Belgium, whose brewers infect their beers with wild yeast and bacteria by cooling their wort in giant pools on the roofs of their breweries.

After a few years of contact in infected wooden barrels, these wild microbes have created a drink somewhere in the middle between beer, cider and wine. We'll learn more about spontaneous fermentation like this is the next chapter.

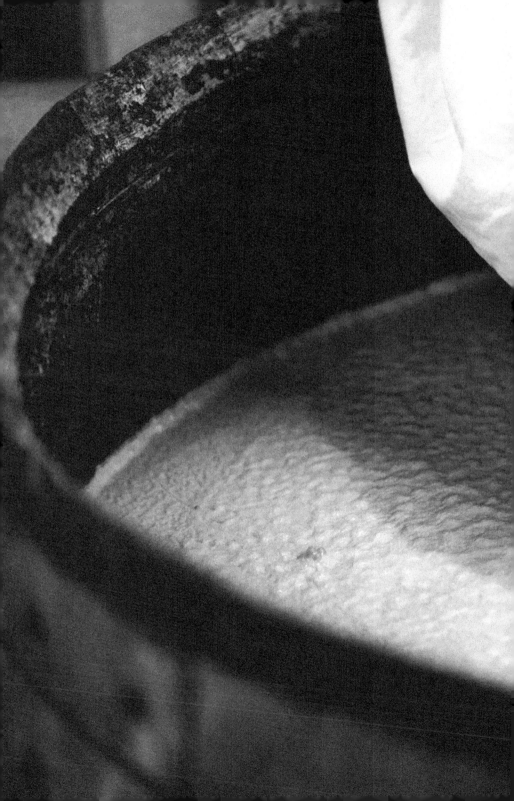

# CHAPTER

# THE FERMENTATION

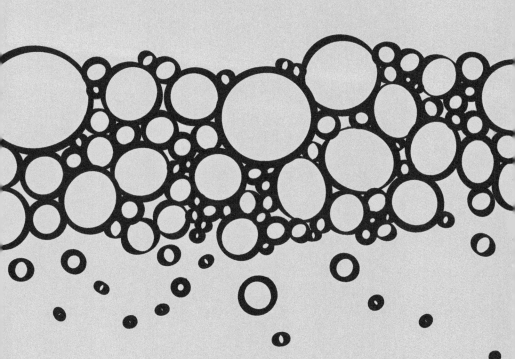

A nd so it all comes down to this. The wort is pumped off into giant, upside-down rockets called fermenters where it will become the beer that was once in the brewer's head. It splashes into the tank, foaming up and taking in lots of oxygen before the yeast is pitched, the swing door secured and the waiting game begins.

Except that implies the process is over. It is, in fact, just beginning. At this point there is no alcohol, the wort is kind of sticky, and there's absolutely no balance to the beer. But in a few weeks it's going to be very different indeed. What happens in the fermenting tank will make or break a beer. It could make all the ingredients sing in perfect harmony or come to clash and create discord. Hops could turn to dust and earth, malts to sticky treacle, and yeast to Marmite. It's up to the brewer to protect it all.

Depending on the style, a beer could stay in these tanks for anything between a week and six months. How long it spends in tank is down to how you'll package it, what yeast strain you're using, and the temperatures the mixture's held at. You see, every yeast has an optimum temperature range and brewers can play within it to achieve what they're after. The higher the temperature, the faster the fermentation and (usually) the more flavour the brewer will extract from the yeast. If you push German weissbier yeast to the max, you'll heighten the lovely banana aroma. If you push saison yeast, more spice might manifest itself. Think of it like an athlete – the harder it works, the more it's going to sweat stuff out.

Ales are pretty much around the two or three week mark between yeast pitching and becoming the finished product. This is because the yeast is operating at a warm temperature, so its metabolism is through the roof. Sometimes literally, as it's not unheard of to see yeast and beer escaping the top of the fermenter and cascading down the sides.

Lagers are a very different beast, though, and fermentation is by far the most critical moment in its life. The term lager derives from the German word "lagern", which means "to store." It refers to when most beers were fermented in caves, which were the only places with the consistently cool temperatures. (This was probably around 10°C or 50°F – much lower than ale yeast would work at.)

So lagers are bottom-fermented beers held at much lower temperatures. This slows down the yeast action and means it metabolises slowly. As we know, yeast fermentation throws out all kinds of weird aromas – some we like and some we don't – but with lagers we want no esters left over at all. The point of a helles and a pilsner is to have the bready malts dominate, balanced by some crisp lemony hops. These are two delicate, sharp flavours that don't want that rounded, fruity yeast characteristic. So not only does the fermentation take longer, but also brewers have to let the beer sit until the yeast starts to eat up the chemical compounds it created at the start of the process.

Bavarian brewers, who know a thing or two about lager, aim for around eight weeks in tank to let the beer's aroma settle. Many brewers give it less time, a sad fact you can usually pick up instantly from the strange, sticky sweetness or even banana-like fruitiness that bad lagers have. By contrast, my favourite lager in the world, Kout 12 from the Czech Republic, is lagered for three whole months – and their dark lager for six!

As always, there are exceptions to this binary ale/lager rule. For example, many strong Belgian ales like Westmalle Tripel are

cool conditioned like a lager so that the sediment slowly drops and clears the beer without having to filter out the good stuff. Meanwhile, some lagers are fermented at ale temperatures to amplify all those messy yeasty flavours and not lagered – the most famous examples of this is the Anchor Steam Beer. The Kolsch lagers of Cologne, Germany, are also fermented in this way before being lagered at low temperatures to get a balance of yeasty esters and crisp, clear flavours.

Working out when it is time to package the beer is pretty easy. The brewers would be taking gravity readings to determine the speed of the fermentation, and when it comes to a stop it probably means the yeast has eaten all the available sugar. Unless the beer needs conditioning (like a lager yeast that needs to clean up the mess it made), the brewer doesn't want to delay because the hops are now on their unstoppable path to destruction. Getting the beer into drinkers hands is now a matter of urgency.

So far in this chapter we have mostly talked about the esters adding to the flavour of beer or indeed distracting us from it. But there are lots more ways that brewers can affect the flavour of a beer while it's fermenting.

# DRY HOPPING

The nerdier among you may have picked up on a bit of a dilemma with long fermentation times. Beer has a limited shelf life, and in nearly all cases should be enjoyed fresh (more on that later). So, surely, if you let your beer hang around in tank it's going to slowly lose flavour.

Well, while a beer is still fermenting and very much alive, it's more helpful to think of it as changing rather than ageing. The brewer is simply waiting for the beer to taste exactly as he or she wants it to. The quicker that happens the better, but you can't rush fermentation. With the beer sat in tank, brewers have all the time in the world to play with flavour, most commonly using my favourite tactic – more hops.

Dry hopping is the act of adding more hops to the fermenter. As we now know, the bittering acids of hops only breakdown at high temperatures, so this is a great point at which to add a load of hop aroma (and some flavour) to the beer without adding to the IBU of the beer. If you've ever opened a beer and been hit by citrus from two feet away, or sniffed a beer and felt like you had your head in a bag of hops, that's probably the insane aroma of a fresh dry-hopped beer.

Dry hopping is common practice in modern craft breweries – some even use "hop cannons" to ensure the hops touch every millilitre of beer – but the practice is ancient, and some less likely breweries use it. The brewers of Brasserie d'Orval in the Trappist Monastery in Belgium use European hops to add a subtle but pithy orange aroma to the beer, which complements the spice and funk of the brett yeast.

This more conservative approach has been thrown out the window, with obscene amounts of hops being added to fermenters. In their usual way, craft brewers have been fascinated with process and tried every way possible to get more aroma into their beer. Brewers on the East Coast of the US in particular believe that adding the hops at the height of fermentation could cause some kind of amalgamation of hop oils, yeast and proteins to carry more hop oil in suspension and improve the flavour. The result is a very cloudy beer, but an almost overwhelmingly juicy hop flavour. It's all part of a shift in hops towards the end of the process, and it's only getting more pronounced.

## SPONTANEOUS FERMENTATION

Not all fermentation happens in giant chrome tanks. There are still hundreds of breweries around the world that ferment their beer in wood. This is significant because where steel is nearly impermeable, wooden fermenting vessels take on the flavours of whatever they contain very quickly – and indeed release flavours into the beer, too.

The most famous example of fermenting in wood can be found in the lambic producers. Funky, fruity, dry and sour, these beers are some of the most complex and highly prized in the world – and with good reason.

It starts with the wort, which throws all the rules of the mash out of the window by using up to 60% wheat, (effectively) two mash tuns and sometimes going on for four hours. The beer is boiled with aged hops (purely for preservative power) then, rather than being mixed with cultivated yeast, it is poured into giant swimming pools at the top of the brewery, where it slowly cools in the open air and gets infected with the unique microflora of the local area.

The inoculated wort is pumped into barrels, some older than the brewers who handle them, where the beer is left for up to three years. In contrast to the fast fermenting ales of the modern world, lambic beers are slow, gentle beers. Like the wort itself, these ancient barrels are imbued with all sorts of flavours, bacteria and yeasts. It takes a long time for them to convert the

sugar, but boy does it convert it. The mix of sacchronomyces and hungry brett pretty much wipe out all sweetness from the beer, so much so that most released versions are blends of young and old lambics to get the balance of the sweeter wheat beer and the funky cider notes. Such a blend is called a gueuze, and it's a hugely complicated beer that has as much in common with scrumpy cider as it does with beer. Another way to round out lambic is to age it over fruits like cherry (krieks), raspberry (framboise) or lots more exciting ingredients.

This style of brewing is absurdly difficult to get right. Jean van Roy of Cantillon may call it "the most natural beer in the world," but that's easy for him to say. He grew up amongst the barrels helping his father. Creating the environment for these beers to thrive is very hard without the natural attributes of the Pajottenland, and the Belgian lambics are largely untouchable in the world of spontaneous fermented beers.

## BARREL AGEING

Those inspired by Belgian sours aren't the only people using wood to infuse their beers with flavour. British styles have been stored in the wood for centuries in an artful process that all but died out before the craft beer revolution. Now, "beer from the wood" is the kind of thing bearded sandal-wearers travel miles for with their notepads and half-moon spectacles at the ready (in my head at least). But there is a new obsession with wood started by the Americans, or more precisely the Chicagoans of Goose Island Brewing Company.

This brewery was, reputedly, the first to age their beers in spirit barrels. They teamed up with the awesome Jim Beam distillery after learning that their barrels were destroyed after one use.

Head brewer Greg Hall saw both the waste and the opportunity here. They brewed a truly massive imperial stout and added it to the spent bourbon whisky barrels. The resulting beer went on to become one of the most sought-after and famous in the world.

Since then, thousands of breweries across the world have started barrel-ageing programmes, expanding out to scotch, white and red wine, port, sherry and even tequila barrels in a bid to add more nuanced (or occasionally very ballsy) flavours to their beers. As well as adding the more obvious oak and alcohol flavours, barrels can add acidity, through bacteria or brett, and more unlikely characters from the wood, such as coconut and vanilla, which are native to the fibres of the original tree. Barrels, whether for souring or ageing, are perhaps the place where nature still has the strongest grip on a brewer's hand, leading him as much as he steers it.

But the thing that brewers can least control in brewing is what happens once the beer is finished and it's shipped out. The remainder of this book is about exactly that – how best to care for, serve and enjoy beer.

# CHAPTER

# SERVING

L et's get one thing straight: there is no "best way" to serve beer, so don't let anyone tell you there is. Every style has its own ideal way of serving, whether it's from a keg, cask, can or bottle. Even then any supposed ideal is pretty subjective.

In the UK there has been keg versus cask mentality ever since the Campaign for Real Ale (CAMRA) started their crusade against bland keg beers in the 1970s. In those dark times it was a valid argument. Rubbish continental pasteurised lagers were taking over the bar at the expense of traditional ales. These local beers were on cask, a serving system that had been used in the UK for centuries. They were part of the UK's history, but they were being forced out by the capitalist pressures of economies of scale.

You can tell a cask beer because it's usually hand pumped up from the cellar rather than poured from a pressurised tap. Most importantly, it's delivered to the pub still fermenting, so the barman can put it on when it's at its absolute peak. That living product, fresh as can be, bore no resemblance to the desperately dull keg lagers and bitters coming up through the ranks thanks to clever marketing by corporate macrobrewers. The British cask ale would have all but died out if it weren't for a few young enthusiasts who went from (presumably) the kind of drunken pub rant we've all been part of to a national campaign that changed the course of British beer.

CAMRA will always be heroes to beer lovers in Britain. The fact that a bunch of beer nerds managed to stand up to huge commercial pressure from giant companies is worthy of everyone's admiration. But fast-forward 40 years and keg beer is a very different beast. There is still the dumbed down pale lager, but there is also a vast array of unpasteurised, exciting keg beer that couldn't be more different to macrolager if it tried (and it will never stop trying).

Good keg beer came into being thanks to the West Coast of America, where homebrewers were taking cues from traditional British ales but adding their new citrusy hops to them. In 1970s America, keg beer was basically all they knew, so everything went into pressurised keg. That's what led to keg beer having a complete monopoly over the US craft beer market. America has perhaps the greatest beer scene in the world, but the lack of cask is a damned shame because many of its lovely beers could be better if served on cask.

Cask versus keg is a hugely personal matter, which is why no one can agree which is best. Some people find the serving temperature of cask (around 11°C) a little bit warm for a beer, while others dislike the fact that the natural carbonation will never tickle the taste buds like a pressurised beer.

These two variations are key to why cask can be so great, and equally not so great, for a beer. The colder something is the less your palate can break down the flavours, so drinking a beer slightly warmer will open it up and let the aromas and flavours really shine. By the same token, high carbonation can be a little distracting on the palate, so a less carbonated beer is easier to dissect.

Sounds great doesn't it? So why on earth would we drink keg? Well, the carbonation that is distracting on the palate actually gets the aromas of the beer right up in your grill, so if you've got a hoppy beer screaming tropical fruit, a keg is going to do it more justice. Drinking a cooler beer is obviously more refreshing on a hot day (not something us Brits have to worry about often), but it can also make the beer seem lighter on its

feet. Malt flavours seem bright, the alcohol sweetness is more balanced and the bitterness is less tannic.

You can see how this makes some beers more suited to certain mediums, and they usually follow their historical origins. Stouts, porters, bitters and ESBs are usually best on cask because their malty richness and body are emphasised. IPAs, pale lagers and berlinerweisses are usually best on keg because their lighter bodies and fresh aromas can leap out of the glass and dance off your palate. Falling into the middle ground would be beers like barley wines and black IPAs where a keg might make the aromas sing and lighten the sticky bodies, but a cask could make their dark, brooding flavours all the more exciting. In these situations we put our trust in the brewer and his or her intentions. If you are brewing a beer for cask, then you might lower the ABV to stop it getting sticky or up the hops so they still stand out. Brewing for keg, you might use a little caramalt to add some depth and make sure the sweetness shows at the lower temperature.

It's a sad fact, though, that cask has one major disadvantage. Because it is a living product when delivered to the pub, the brewer is handing over control of the final and very important part of the process – the conditioning. In a good pub it means the beer is served as soon as it is ready, and in all probability you'll taste the beer at the very best it can be. But if the publican stores the beer too cold or hot, or lets it condition for too long or too short a time, a beer can be ruined. Thus, when drinking cask, we always ask for a taster before buying to make sure the beer has been well looked after by the pub.

# CLARITY OF THOUGHT

Although filtering happens at the brewery between the fermenter and the packaging, it's at the point of serving where the question is always asked: "Is this beer supposed to be cloudy?"

Potential brewing flaws aside, the answer is "yes." While there is something hugely appetising about a crystal clear beer, there is not a lot to recommend it. When you filter a beer, you are stripping flavour and, to some extent, body. There is an argument as to whether you want those flavours in the beer, but I think our obsession with clarity is mostly a hangover from cask beer, when clarity was one sign of a beer being conditioned and ready to serve in the pub. This was because the sediment slowly dropped out, and this rule is still true unless the beer is never meant to clarify and is full of hoppy goodness.

These days a little bit of haze is probably a good sign. Heavily dry-hopped beers often get what is called "hop haze", where the sheer amount of hop oils add a cloudy shimmer to the beer. The hop oils can also interact with the malt proteins to form a haze in all hoppy beers, particularly at lower temperatures. Neither phenomenon is a brewing flaw and both excite me because, aside from aroma, it's the surest sign of a beer having hops. Lots of hops.

Knowing that they may be stripping out flavour and trusting that people are coming round to the idea of hazy beer, in the last few years brewers have started leaving their beers unfined and even purposefully brewing murky beer.

This has been taken to extremes by the brewers of East Coast IPAs, who use lots of high protein grains like wheat and oats to make their beers utterly opaque. The theory is that, when dry hopped early during fermentation, the yeast, hops and malt proteins will band together and suspend in the beer to result in the juiciest, cloudiest and smoothest beer possible.

But it's not just the trendy east coasters who love opaque beers. Germans, and later Belgians, have long been producing ultra-murky beers loaded with yeast and wheat to get the silkiest, flavour-laden beer they can.

Of course, many beers are indeed better when finely filtered – most lagers want a crisper, more focused finish, and very bitter IPAs are often more spiky and citrusy when cleaned up – but, to us, a little hop haze is a beautiful thing.

# SHOULD YOU BOTTLE IT UP?

You'd think when it comes to bottled beer things would be simpler. Sadly, they're not. The arguments aren't quite as heated as those about cask versus keg, but like anything on the internet if you search hard enough, you'll find the angry people.

Luckily, there are some certainties to cling on to. There are three enemies of beer – light, heat and oxygen. Light and heat are the destroyers of flavour, the bringers of the "hopocalypse." They break down the volatile hop oils that give us all that juiciness, dankness and fresh hop aroma. What they leave behind smells vaguely like marijuana, but also a lot like dust. This process is known as being "lightstruck", and eventually, it ruins all hoppy beers. The best way to protect against it is to use brown glass, which filters out the offending spectrum of light – any beer served in green or clear glass ain't worth the time it takes to open one. An even better way to protect the beer is to put it in a can, which lets no light in at all. Because it's metal, and metal doesn't let in any light.

So if cans are the best way to protect a beer from damage, then why aren't all beers in cans? The man reason is stigma – the fact that the macros realised the benefits first meant a lot of bad beer went into can, ruining the format for everyone. Thankfully, that is starting to change as brave craft breweries take the plunge and consumers realise the can's benefits.

But here is where the debate begins, because there is a potential flaw in the can. The third, and most insidious, enemy of beer is oxygen. When a beer gets oxidised it can gain a horrible, damp sweetness that slowly turns to a cardboard-like staleness. Oxygen gets into the bottle as you fill it, and the mark of a really great bottling machine is how little oxygen sneaks in.

This is reduced by purging the bottle with carbon dioxide, and it's relatively easy to do with its ring-sized aperture. With a can, though, there is much greater chance of the beer getting oxidised both through the larger aperture of the opening and the less reliable seal.

So the choice for a brewery is either potentially compromising the beer while packaging, or letting light compromise it in a bottle. You can see why the internet forums ignite when someone poses the question.

There is one final variable to throw into the mix. That variable is bottle conditioning. Many breweries carbonate their beers before they go into bottle by pumping carbon dioxide into the beer like a Soda Stream. Others do it more naturally by fermenting under pressure in the tank, which pushes the carbon dioxide produced by the yeast into the beer. The third option is to do the same thing in the bottle. By adding a little sugar and/or yeast to the bottle (or can), you can kick off a final fermentation that carbonates the beer in the bottle. This makes CAMRA very happy because they don't like the idea of force carbonating. But more importantly it means the fermentation is eating up the oxygen in the bottle. This protects the beer from oxidation for longer, even if it means you have to pour a little more carefully to avoid a spoonful of yeast sediment in your beer.

What it can also do is help the beer age well. With the extended shelf life that bottle conditioning can give, we create the opportunity for the beer to change and evolve in the bottle. Sound exciting? Read on.

# CHAPTER

# STORING

**W**hen we buy an item of food and bring it home, we all check the label to see where it should be stored. Should it be in the fridge? A cool, dark place? Can it just sit on the side? No one does that with beer, but they should.

What we learnt in the last chapter about the three main enemies of beer should make it obvious how to store it. Whatever the style, it needs to be kept in a place that is dark, consistent and chilled. A fridge is perfect, but a cool spot in the garage might work or, if you're that kind of person, the wine cellar. I have my own beer fridge at home full of bottles with no food allowed. I keep it at a regular 8°C/46°F, so my beer isn't so cold that it suppresses flavours or so warm that it's not refreshing.

So all beer should be stored cold and out of sunlight. That much is clear. But the most common mistake people make in the storing of their beer is that they actually store it at all.

Food producers (and let's face it, beer is liquid bread) are legally required to put a "best before" date on their packaging. In most cases this is a guess at when the food might start to stale or even go off. Because beer is alcoholic, it doesn't really go off. Instead it changes – and it starts changing from the moment it's put in the bottle. The longer it's lived and the further it's travelled, the less it will taste like the beer in the brewer's head.

Packaging in brown bottles or cans and storing it right will help ensure you get a beautiful beer, but the best way to do it is to drink it fresh. Some breweries put a year on their beers, others six months, and some just three. But there is a lot to be said for drinking them even fresher. I promise you, it doesn't take an experienced palate to tell the difference between a week-old beer and a six-month old beer. There is a vibrancy to brewery-fresh beer that is hard to overstate, especially in lagers and hoppier beers. I like to compare it to the difference between just-baked bread and that same loaf the next day. In fact, if I could give a new beer lover one piece of advice it would be to store properly and drink fresh. The difference can be revelatory.

The exception, of course, is if you want to age a beer.

That's right, age it. Just like fine wine, many beer styles can be aged. There is already a market for vintage beers, with bottles going for absurd prices. I'm not sure how I feel about that, but I can vouch for the fact that, carefully looked after, an aged beer can blow your mind just as much as an absurdly fresh one.

Before we get into the intricacies of beer cellaring, though, it's important to remember that very few beers will age well. Some are never born to be aged – hop-forward beers and delicate styles like pale lager will never improve once bottled or canned. There are lots of studies being done by breweries on their beers, but inside the bottle there is a whole ecosystem at work and myriad chemical processes we still don't fully understand (aside from the loss of hoppy aroma and flavour).

There are two main forces at play in this ecosystem – oxygen and yeast. For that reason, you probably shouldn't age anything that isn't bottle conditioned. Without yeast eating the oxygen, it will slowly oxidise and those cardboard-like flavours will come to dominate the beer.

If it is bottle conditioned, though, the yeast can thrive, eating up the additional sugar and oxygen and throwing out lots of extra alcohol and esters. If the yeast is having fun, these esters can totally change the beer. Studies have found that the more classic esters like banana and clove will fade and be replaced by unusual

ones that can have whisky and wine-like qualities. This explains why many people have described an aged beer as "port-like." What is port if not a rounded, sweeter wine? Well, ageing beer has a similar effect, bringing out sweetness in a bitter liquid and adding spirit-like depth. Conversely, the alcohol "heat" is likely to dissipate relative to the new flavours coming out, so we can add alcohol depth while removing any burn. This is all starting to sound exciting, right?

You may have noticed a limiting factor, though. Once the oxygen and sugar are gone, surely oxidation will start to take hold and the positive changes will be slowly lost. This is true, and only the very best and strongest beers will benefit from more than a year's ageing. But for some very special bottles the rules are broken, and this is where things get less scientific and more mysterious. You see, beer ages in cycles. Take three bottles of Belgian quad. At one year you might find it medicinal, bitter and unbalanced. But wait another six months and you'll find another bottle rich in raisins, dates and port-like sweet acidity. Wait yet another six months and you could be back where you started.

It seems the yeast, or at least its effects, come in waves, and there is some reaction causing these chemicals to bond at one point then release at others. I remember going to a talk about beer ageing with the great Jon Keeling of Fuller's Brewery, and even he couldn't give straight answers about what is going on in the bottle. However, what he could do with his immense experience is tell us the best ways to age our beers and drink them at their peak. I humbly pass these methods on with some extra advice from my experience of trying to run my own cellar (I mean beer fridge).

# THE GOLDEN RULES

- Buy a few bottles so you can try them at different ages. Drink one immediately, for obvious reasons (because it's tasty).

- Pick a quality beer with lots of alcohol and malty flavours, ideally with interesting yeast strains because these will develop most over time.

- Remember flavours round out while ageing, so go for big, rich flavours. Toffee, coffee and chocolate will keep their impact. Lemon, pineapple and banana might change.

- Keep the beer away from direct light, and preferably any light at all.

- Don't let the beers warm up past about 25°C/77°F. That's where bad stuff really starts to happen. Ideally keep it around 14°C/57°F. Essentially, beers should be stored at the temperature at which you'll want to drink them.

- Store your beer upright to avoid contact with the cap or cork. There is no evidence that keeping the cork wet can protect the beer, but there's lots of evidence that contact with a cap can damage a beer.

# BRILLIANT BEERS TO AGE
## (AND WHAT HAPPENS TO THEM)

We've picked five easy-to-find beers we've tried vintages of and know will be delicious.

## ORVAL

This is the cliché when it comes to ageing beer, but with good reason. Orval is a dry-hopped Belgian pale ale (made by Monks, obviously) that is re-fermented in the bottle with brett yeast.

When the beer is fresh, the beer has a sherberty sweetness from the yeast, pithy orange aroma and a lively body. If aged for six months or a little longer, it transforms the beer into a cider-like, farmyard-y beer with huge, challenging aroma but a soft and bittersweet body...until that cider aroma comes back on the aftertaste. It is the Jekyll and Hyde of the beer world: a shapeshifter. And an absolute joy.

## OSKAR BLUES TEN FIDY

When we were invited to a vintage tasting of this beer I was skeptical. What I loved about this beer was how hoppy it was – almost like a black IPA with lots of citrus tempered by a roasted character like a grilled pineapple. I didn't know if ageing this hoppy monster for two years was a good idea.

How wrong I was. The citrus was nearly all gone, replaced by a smooth roasted coffee and dark, dark chocolate with just enough fruity acidity to make for a clean finish. I couldn't say which was better, the fresh or the aged, so best try them both at the same time.

## ROCHEFORT 10

This is one of my favourite beers in the world, and my dream is to one day come across a bottle that has been aged for decades. Instead, I've tried a couple of vintages, the oldest being three years. It was well looked after, because all the flavours you expect in an aged beer were present – heightened sweetness with a port-like boozy edge on the aroma and not a hint of alcohol on the palate.

## FULLER'S VINTAGE ALE

A beer only brewed to be aged, Fuller's Vintage Ale is released in (relatively) small batches every year with annual variations in the recipe – most notably the hop. Otherwise, it is a light-coloured strong ale that is grassy and spicy when fresh but a different beast when aged. I've had a 2014, 2012, 2008 and a 2002 and, unsurprisingly, my favourite was the eldest. It had gained a tequila edge – all oak and spicy booze despite never seeing a cask in its life. On the palate it had marmalade, candied sweets and an orange–pith bitterness.

## BOON KRIEK MARIAGE PARFAIT

Krieks are one of my favourite styles, and this one is perhaps my number one. Here the blenders have added a lot more old lambic to increase the dry cider edge and puckering sourness. It's already an outrageously complex brew when it goes into bottle, but after a year it's gained some sherry tones and a smoother finish to match the rich cherry notes. A mariage parfait indeed.

# CHAPTER

# POURING

Don't fuck it up now. You've come so far. From the mind of the brewer to the mash and boil and fermenter; through hundreds of metres of pipes and hoses into a bottle or can, it's been shipped to you, perhaps from the other side of the world. It's time is near.

The pour is much more important that you might think. The speed, the temperature, the glass – these are all final defining factors in our enjoyment of a beer. Not getting them right is sneering in the face of the brewer. If it's been brewed, packaged and stored right, though, pouring is easy, whatever a Belgian barman might claim about it being an art.

It starts with the temperature. Most beer in this world is either served too warm or too cold but the rules are simple. The warmer something is, the more you can taste it. Macrolagers are served near freezing to hide what little flavour they have, while beers like barley wines tend to be served closer to room temperature, around 14°C. This opens up the complex aromas and flavours so your senses can pick them apart.

Most other styles should be served around the 8°C/46°F mark so they are refreshing but flavourful. The only exception would be cask ale, which is best enjoyed at the cellar temperature of 10–12°C (around 50°F), where it's tingly carbonation and rich flavour is at its strongest. Real ale in bottle, though, is better off lower. A pretty sound rule is to add 2°C to the ABV of the beer, but I'd never serve anything below 5°C.

With those universal rules agreed, we're now all about speed, which dictates the head and the sediment. For some reason, most drinkers are averse to a healthy head on a beer. Maybe they think they aren't getting their money's worth, but they're wrong. What they lose in quantity they get tenfold in quality. A good head releases aroma, protects the beer from oxygen and is, in fact, the sign of a well-made beer. For most styles, we think about an inch of head is right. It's enough to get all the benefits without dipping your nose when you swoop in for a sip.

As usual, not everyone agrees with us. In the Czech Republic the most common Pilsner pour is the "hladinka" – served in a small handle glass with one-third head to two-thirds beer to make for a deliciously creamy beer. The head of Bohemian lager is designed to stick around, and it lasts the whole way down the glass to keep the beer protected. I've even heard stories of drinkers in Pilsen discarding away their beer as soon as the head disappears because the liquid is then compromised.

An extreme version of that bubbly pour is the "mliko" pour – all head and no liquid. Obviously it takes a special, tight and smooth head to make this an appetising prospect, but with Pilsner Urquell it is a revelation, like breathing in a bittersweet cloud.

In Germany an inch head is usually the least you'll be poured, and that's fine with us – there's nothing like a beard covered in wheat beer – but it's in Belgium where the real hedonists reside, pouring their beers fast then artfully swiping aside the extra head with the flick of a bar blade. As well as ensuring a healthy head, it makes the pour more of an event – something to be watched and admired, rather than a slightly impatient wait while being jostled at the bar.

And there's another area in which the Belgian barkeeps are king...

# HOW TO POUR

**1**   HOLD THE GLASS AT A 45° ANGLE, THEN TIP THE BOTTLE UNTIL BEER FALLS INTO THE GLASS

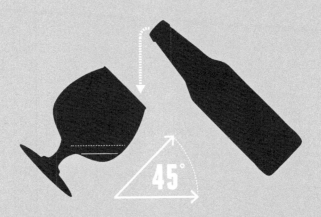

**2**   TO INCREASE THE HEAD, MOVE THE BOTTLE UPWARDS RATHER THAN TILT THE BOTTLE MORE TO KEEP THE YEAST SEDIMENT IN THE GLASS

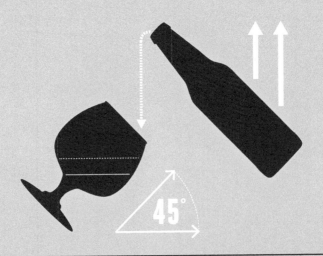

**3** ONCE YOU START POURING TRY NOT TO STOP OR YOU WILL MIX THE YEAST INTO THE BEER

**4** NEVER LET THE BOTTLE GO PAST HORIZONTAL BECAUSE THE NECK IS CATCHING THE SEDIMENT

**5** GRADUALLY MAKE THE GLASS VERTICAL LEAVING AROUND AN INCH OF HEAD

# GLASSWARE

If there is one thing I want you to take from this section, it's that you stop using straight and conical pint glasses. They are without the doubt the least suitable and ridiculous drinking vessel ever devised. Hell, I'd rather drink from a colander.

There is literally nothing to recommend a pint glass other than habit. It is too wide for you to get decent aroma from it, it's too thick to chill down with the beer, and it's too big to suit stronger beers. The glass was designed purely to survive the onslaught of drunken abuse and hot dishwashers. It does nothing to enhance the drinking experience or the beer it holds, but there are lots of receptacles that do.

The general rule is that you want a bowl shape and a thin mouth to trap the aromas, and preferably a stem so you don't warm the beer with your excitable, sweaty hands. There are loads of glass designs, some shaped by centuries of tradition and others scientifically modeled using a mix of chemistry and modern aesthetics. We have the complete set. Those who drink regularly from them always have a favourite, but each is best suited to a certain style or time.

## FROM THE BOTTLE

I get it. Drinking from the bottle is pretty awesome. You get no aromas – you might as well hold your nose – and the beer can get awfully warm very quickly, but when you need a beer and can just crack it and swig, well that's one of the best feelings in the world. Tilt away, my friends (just not with an imperial stout).

# FROM THE CAN

There's a scene in the Truman Show where Truman starts to question his very existence. The Truman Show producer's response is to get his "best friend" to come round with a six pack of cans, head to the lake in a pick up and talk it all out. Aside from the fact Truman's best friend is lying through his teeth, every facet of this scene makes me pine for an American nostalgia I've never known. Damn, if sharing a six pack with a friend isn't the definition of happiness, then I don't know what is.

# GERMAN HANDLED MASS

Tall and thin, these lager glasses are much better for aroma than a normal pint glass while still being satisfying to drink from. In fact, one of my best beer experience was drinking Augustiner Helles on cask from a 500ml maß in Munich. With a towering white head, it was filled in three seconds flat, and drunk nearly as fast.

# WEISSBIER GLASS

There is no other word for it – weissbier glasses are sexy, shapely things. The slight bowl shape means you can really get your head in that lovely, ester-y atmosphere. The thin bottom means you warm up the minimum amount of beer with your hands, but it also encourages you to finish the pint quickly.

# PILSNER GLASS

Quite where these came from is a mystery – tall, thin, pointless. They warm up too fast and don't help with aroma at all.

# GLASSWARE

 CHALICE

 IPA

 SNIFTER

 TULIP

 TEKU

# CHOOSE YOUR WEAPON

GUEZE

DIMPLE

PINT

WEISSBIER

MAß

PILSNER

# GUEZE GLASS

I love the feel of these heavy-bottomed conicals. They aren't ideal for aroma but the aromas of lambics is so strong you'll know exactly what's going on. The heavy base is due to the fact that the first lambics would have had a spoonful of sugar crushed in before drinking to mellow the sourness. The chunky feel means they are very satisfying to drink from, and a huge part of the experience of drinking lambic in Belgium.

# CHALICE

Walk into a good Belgian beer bar and you will see a very big and confusing beer fridge. Even I can get lost in all the beers I have neither seen nor heard of before. But the most amazing thing is that the majority of these beers will have their own glass, and even more amazingly the bar will whip one out of nowhere when you order. Having the right glass is essential to proud Belgian beer lovers, and I've even been told I couldn't have an Orval in a bar because there were no glasses left.

Now, being objective for a moment, chalices aren't great for getting the aroma of a beer. Sometimes the mouth of the glass is as wide as your face. But for some reason I can't enjoy an Orval from any other glass, and Westmalle in anything but the official goblet feels like sacrilege.

# TULIP GLASS

A great all-purpose glass, this style can come in many sizes. The subtle bowl shape and thin mouth are ideal for appraising beers, and the smaller sizes are great for high ABV beers.

# SNIFTER GLASS

Another great glass for all styles, but traditionally used for Belgian strong ales. The big bowl traps all the lovely esters of this style, and it can do the same for hop aromas, too. It has the bonus of making you feel like a British duke.

# TEKU

Perhaps the most over-engineered glass in the history of forever, the teku is designed to have the widest bowl possible with the thinnest mouth opening – and it really does concentrate the aromas. Brilliant for strong beers or intense wild beers that you need to dissect.

# IPA GLASS

I love these glasses. You get the wide bowl and thin top, but the thin bottom segment does an awesome job of making the beer slop over itself and regenerate the head, so you have a frothy pint right to the last few sips.

# PINT GLASS

Down quickly or decant into a wine glass.

# DIMPLE JUG

Much like the pint glass, this is useless as a beer receptacle, but holding a dimple jug and drinking cask ale is a quintessentially British experience that I won't begrudge anyone.

# CHAPTER

**13**

# TASTING

S ome beers should be served cold and slung back. Others are meant to be sipped slowly while being considered, ideally with the odd beard scratch and quizzical side-eye.

Neither kind is better than the other. Perhaps my favourite beer of all time, Kout 12, is a lager that definitely falls into the sling 'em back category...once you get over the insane spicy caramel aroma, that is. But there is nothing like taking a barley wine, Belgian quad or imperial IPA and really taking it to pieces. Working out what influence the hops, malt and yeast have had, what the brewer meant and what he achieved, and whether it's the best beer in the world or just another hyped up IPA. That, in short, is the role of the beer judge, and the joy is that we can all learn to be one.

Your palate is a complicated instrument and totally unique from everyone else's, so there is no right or wrong when it comes to tasting beer. There's a reason why beer competitions use so many judges – bias, personality, experience and sensitivities all affect how we perceive a beer's aroma and flavour. All you need to know are the best ways to release and appraise them. This is our guide to tasting beer like a beer judge, and we know it's good because we learnt it from Ray Daniels, the founder of the Cicerone accreditation scheme himself.

The first thing you need to do is get the right glass. As we learnt in the last chapter, there are all kinds of glasses that bring out the best in different styles. The best generic one is the aptly named snifter, and it is a lot like a brandy glass. We also think a teku is very good at this job. From here, though, the most important piece of equipment is your nose.

# HOW TO TASTE

## THE PASS
PASS THE BEER REPEATEDLY PAST YOUR NOSE AT SHOULDER HEIGHT TO GET THE STRONG AROMAS

  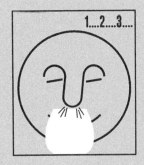

## THE BLOODHOUND
SWILL THE BEER, GET YOUR NOSE IN THE GLASS AND GIVE IT THREE SHARP SNIFFS

 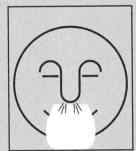 

## THE HEADY SNIFF
SWILL THE BEER, GET YOUR NOSE IN THE GLASS AND INHALE DEEPLY. SMILE

## THE COVERED SNIFF
Cover the glass with a hand and swill the beer, then repeat the heady sniff

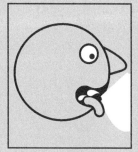

## THE SIP
Enough to coat and not to float the tongue

## GOING RETRO
Swallow, breath out through your nose. Dive in again

# BREAKING DOWN A BEER

There are three techniques to get the most out of the aroma of a beer, and you should use all three to make sure you have approached the beer from every angle. Fill the glass with beer to about one-third. Before each step, make sure you swirl the beer around for a few seconds to release the aromas. If you're unsure, refer to the previous page.

## UNDER THE NOSE

For the first sniff, you're going to simply wave the glass under your nose from around shoulder height. You'll be surprised by how much aroma you perceive from that distance. This is because many beers have one particular characteristic that stands out and dominates. It could be grapefruit from the hops, banana from the yeast or chocolate from the malt. Whatever it is, it's likely to either mask the other aromas or overwhelm you palate. Think of it like when you cook fish in the house – eventually, you adapt and don't notice the smell, but if you leave and come back, BOOM! There it is. This technique lets you pick up and pick apart those huge aromas so you don't miss them or the more subtle ones later.

## BLOODHOUND TECHNIQUE

If you've ever watched a dog on the trail of something, you'll have noticed that they don't take great long sniffs as they go. Actually, they take short, sharp sniffs in quick succession. This is because your nose is most sensitive to a change in aroma. Taking three or four sniffs means recirculating air and being able to reappraise it each time. You'll be able to find all the beautiful intricacies in the beer, and indeed all the off-flavours...

## THE LONG SNIFF

Now we move on to a technique most of us use without thinking. It's a good two-second sniff that gets the beer right up in your headspace, filling your palate, sinuses and brain with those incredible aromas. You'll get an overall feel for the beer and the interplay of the malt, hops and yeast to help you work out which dominate and which stay in the background.

## THE COVERED SNIFF

You're probably getting pretty thirsty by now (not to mention knocking all the bubbles out of your beer), so there is just one more to try if you still feel like there is more to be extracted from the aroma. The covered sniff is exactly as described. This time, swirl to release the aromas, but trap them by covering the top of the glass with your hand. Bring the glass up to your nose and remove your hand before taking a long sniff. Usually, you'll pick up the danker, tropical and more intense hop aromas as well as more subtle off-flavours such as sulfur.

## FLAVOUR

Aroma is a huge amount of what we taste, so it is little wonder we spend so much time appraising how a beer smells before we dive in. But finally, it is time to take a sip – enough to coat, but not float, the tongue. Move it around the mouth to make sure the entire palate gets a look in before swallowing. Essentially, you're looking to confirm what you perceived on the aroma – are the hints of dark chocolate or mango or clove still there? You're also looking for things your nose can't detect – carbonation, mouthfeel, and the all-important bitterness. It might take a few sips to work it all out (shame), but many of these flavours can build with each sip, so you'll get a better sense of the beer the more you drink.

## RETRO-NASAL APPRECIATION

Sounds sexy, doesn't it? Well, this is a technique you might well use subconsciously. It's the act of breathing in as you drink and then breathing out via your nose after swallowing. What this does is send the aromas back through your nasal passage on the way out, and it's a really important part of tasting food (which explains why we can hardly taste anything when we have a blocked nose). Breathing out after drinking can bring all kinds of aromas back in sharper focus, as well as create the fullest sense of a beer. Those aromas mingle with our sense of bitterness, sweetness, sourness, saltiness and umami from the tongue.

Of course, once you have swirled until you're dizzy, sniffed until you've sneezed and sipped until satisfied, all that's left to do is sit back and enjoy the beer. For every moment you spend taking a beer apart there should be ten for just relaxing and drinking with friends. For all the wonder of brewing, the greatest achievement of the brewer is to create something that brings people together and makes them happy. We love tasting like a beer judge, but we love drinking great beer even more. So never forget to sit back and relax with one once you're done being a nerd.

# CHAPTER

# EPILOGUE

I didn't get any answers at Treehouse. I just got a new favourite IPA and a whole load more questions, but that was more than worth the drive.

All the answers we have went into this book, which is defined as much by what is in it as what was left out. There are so many details, complications and equations that no book could ever hope to contain them all. In a way, I hope we've given you as many questions as solutions, because the great thing about beer is that most of the answers are found at the bottom of a glass.

We called this book Beer School for a very good reason. The point of school is to prepare you for later life. It is supposed to give you the skills and the motivation to get out there and succeed. It will teach you how to write, but it can't tell you what to write. It gives you a shove in the right direction and leaves the rest up to you.

That's what this book was designed to do. It teaches you to ask the right questions and how to understand the answers. It allows you to go up to the bar and walk away with a good beer in your hand, because even today that's not always guaranteed. Our mission with the Craft Beer Channel is help people enjoy beer, and education is key to that. Some people might say we take it all too seriously, that we should shut up and just have a beer. But the more we know the more we can relax and enjoy that beer. If we know it's hops doing this or yeast doing that, then we can forget about it and enjoy the experience. If we don't understand beer, then we end up questioning it. Think of all the people you know who don't like how bitter beer is, or won't touch sour beer, or think 8% is too strong for a beer. Some education could open their minds and change the way they drink forever.

We hope we've given you enough knowledge to sit back, crack a beer and relax. Just as importantly, we hope you'll be able to pass it on to people who are just getting started on their beery adventure.

We kind of sold you a lie in the introduction. We said that beer was a journey. That's true, but it's not a linear line from A to B. It's a circle we're all going around, waving at each other from the other side. When I'm obsessed with lambics, Brad's addicted to IPAs. When I'm over lager, Brad can't stand stouts. Around we go with no finishing point. Or pint.

Like all the best journeys, you forget the destination on the way. I'm not sure there ever was one for us; it was just about being on the road. We saw a turning, took it and it's led us all over the world. We've visited breweries literally growing from the ruins of Cold War oppression; we've seen small towns revived by new craft businesses, and we've drunk with microbrewers in the Arctic Circle. There have been wrong turns, extended pee breaks and hitchhikers on the way – some have joined permanently, sitting gently drunken in the backseat (Hi, Sam!). We still don't know where we're going, and that's the fun of it. We never pretend to have the all answers or the directions, and you shouldn't either.

We've given you the keys, but everyone's journey is different. Think about your ultimate beer experience – I already know two things about it. One, it will be very different to mine, which proves there is no common end to the beer journey. Two, that one day you'll have an ever better moment that replaces it, which means your journey is never over.

When we started the Craft Beer Channel we were after one thing – an excuse to drink more beer. What we got was a lot more, and there's a lot still to come.

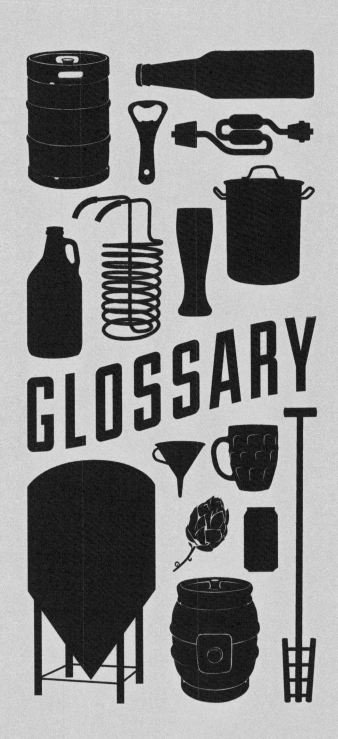

GLOSSARY

Here's a list of words you might not understand or might have mixed up. It covers brewing techniques, beer styles and incomprehensible buzzwords that nerds like us like to trot out to keep the rest of the world guessing.

**ABV (ALCOHOL BY VOLUME):** How drunk you're gonna get, in percentage points.

**ADJUNCT:** An ingredient in beer other than the standard four of barley or wheat, water, hops, and yeast. It could be maize, chocolate, citrus peel, or the brewer's car keys if he's not careful.

**AMERICAN PALE ALE:** The beer that launched a thousand ships. Pale and bittersweet like a British pale ale of old but with a big hit of citrusy hops, all while keeping it sessionable. Pioneered by Sierra Nevada Brewing Company.

**BEER GEEK:** Key indicators include: a plaid jacket, a gilet with a notebook in it, a T-shirt featuring a brewery you've never heard of, a look of disgust when someone orders a lager, sweat that smells of citra hops, a beer belly out of proportion with the rest of their body, a bandana or just a neck beard.

**BERLINERWEISS:** This sour wheat beer has a lemon-barley edge to it. In Germany it is often served with a green or red sugary syrup added, but this is totally disgusting. Thankfully, craft brewers have starting adding more natural ingredients—such as citrus peel and juices—to add depth and excitement to this hugely refreshing style of beer.

**BITTER:** A traditional British style of ale dominated by the fruit and toffee notes of the malts and a little by the stone fruit and banana of the yeast. Hops provide a clean finish. This beer is often served on keg in the US, but it is far superior in a well-kept cask.

**BLACK IPA**: A matter of great debate – can a pale ale be black?! No. No it can't. But we believe the point of a black IPA is clear – take the big citrus aroma of an IPA and balance it with the roasty chocolate of a stout or porter. Devilishly difficult to make, but the good ones are complex, broody and exciting.

**BOIL**: When the wort is heated to boiling point and the hops are added at various times to achieve certain flavours and aromas.

**CONDITIONING**: At the end of fermentation, the yeast has usually thrown up all sorts of unwanted compounds with bad flavours. While the yeasty action is mostly over, it will start to re-process these chemicals to reduce their impact. In lagers, this can take a good few weeks to get the smoothest beer possible. Lagering like this usually takes place in tank (or "bright tanks").

Conditioning can also refer to the clarification of beer in kegs and casks before serving, as well as to the natural carbonation in bottles, where the final throes of fermentation naturally adds carbon dioxide to the liquid under pressure.

**CRAFT BEER**: Oh god, here we go. It must be made by a brewery making no more than 6,000,000 barrels a year, who aren't more than 25% owned by another company that isn't a craft brewer itself, mostly using traditional or innovative techniques, brewing only in the shadows of a full moon using a golden brewing paddle cast in the fires of Kilimanjaro by the anointed High Priest of Exhausting Red Tape.

We get that there needs to be a definition for tax reasons and to protect independent businesses, but good beer is good beer. So let's not get hung up on it as drinkers.

**DOUBLE/IMPERIAL IPA**: A stronger version of the world-famous IPA. It's unlikely to use twice the ingredients, as some claim, but it might just be twice as good.

**DUBBEL**: A strong, dark Belgian beer made famous by its inventor, Westmalle Abbey. Delicious notes of toffee, banana, raisins and rum make it a fantastic winter beer and perfect for ageing.

**EAST COAST IPA**: A style we are completely obsessed with, this near-opaque, yeasty IPA confounds and infuriates purists around the world. Made using a special technique of hopping the beer while fermentation is still happening, these beers are fruitier and smoother than their dank West Coast counterparts. Traditionalists hate the slight yeast twang and cloudy appearance, but the rest of us don't care and continue to drink some of the best IPAs in the world. Crack a can, drink fresh, and don't mind what anyone else tells you.

**ESTER**: The name for the many chemical byproducts of fermentation. In most cases, these chemicals smell delicious and remind us of something tasty, whether it's bananas, peaches or apple.

**FERMENTATION**: The point of brewing where the sugars from the mash are eaten up by yeast, which in turn kicks out alcohol carbon dioxide and esters.

**FRAMBOISE**: A blended lambic aged in barrel with raspberries for a light, summery tartness.

**GOSE**: Since nearly dying out post WWII, the Gose has made a huge comeback everywhere except its native Germany. It's a sour wheat beer with added salt and coriander, which, I admit, sounds disgusting, but it is in fact delicious once you get your head around it. Moreish, biting but quaffable, it's another traditional German style brought bang up to date by the addition of natural adjuncts.

**GRUIT**: A beer bittered or flavoured with a selection of herbs rather than hops. Common variations have included ginger, juniper, caraway and aniseed. Many beers now use these ingredients, but they rarely do so at the expense of the hops because hops are better.

**GUEZE**: A lambic beer that has been blended to round out the more funky flavours and then bottle conditioned until carbonated. Usually, it's very fizzy with lots of cider, cheddar cheese and white wine acidity. To ensure you have a good one, make sure you drink "oude gueze", which means it has not been sweetened.

**HOPS**: The flower of the hop vine that contains lots of resins and oils that add bitterness, flavour and citric aroma to the beer. Originally used in beer to kill bacteria and extend its shelf life, hops have come a long way. They are a distant cousin of cannabis (but the family have agreed to not to talk to him any more).

**IBU (INTERNATIONAL BITTERING UNIT)**: A slightly flawed measure of how bitter a beer is, calculated using the alpha acids of the hops in a beer and time the hops spend above 79°C/175°F. I say it's flawed because what it can't do is compensate for the fact that lots of sweet crystal malt might reduce the perceived bitterness and lots of chocolate malt will probably increase it. 80IBU is about all a human can taste, so don't be fooled by anything with lots more.

**INDIA PALE ALE**: Originally brewed in Britain (perhaps first in Burton) and shipped to expats in India during the times of the Empire, IPA is now the biggest and trendiest craft beer style thanks to a switch from earthy, spicy British hops to tropical and citric American hops.

**KOELSHIP/COOL SHIP**: The giant swimming pools, found in lambic breweries, where the beer is cooled overnight while exposed to the wild yeasts in the air.

**KRIEK**: A blended lambic aged in barrel with cherries for a deep, fruity sourness.

**LACTOBACILLUS**: A bacteria that lowers the pH of a beer and turns it sour. It's a vital ingredient for brewing kettle sours, lambics and berlinerweiss.

**LAMBIC**: Beer made using wild yeasts and bacteria that infect the liquid while cooling in the open air. This liquid is fermented and barrel aged for up to 3 years, then can either be served flat (usually from a pewter jug) or blended, sometimes with fruits.

Debates rage (mostly on Twitter) about whether spontaneously fermented beers made outside of its homeland of Pajottenland can be called lambic, but officially only the process of this style is protected, not the geography.

**LIQUOR**: Just the techie word for water in a brewery.

**MALT**: Germinated and kilned barley (or other brewing grain) that contains the sugar for converting into alcohol at fermentation. It is also responsible for sweet and savoury flavours in beer – from biscuits and honey to toast and chocolate.

**MASH**: The early part of the brew where grains are mixed with hot water and stirred to extract sugar, flavour and colour for the beer.

**MILD**: No one really knows what this beer is. Some say it should be low ABV, but it could be as high at 6%. Some say it should be dark, but others brew lighter brown ones. Some say it should be very lightly hopped while others just can't help themselves. Originally, it was a low-ABV, sweet and malty beer, usually on the dark side of brown to contrast the drier and stronger bitters.

**PAJOTTENLAND**: The region of Belgium with the perfect mix of bacteria and yeast in the air for lambic production.

**PORTER**: Brewed as a hearty beer for the ruddy, overworked porters of London's docks, this beer is rich, warming and fruity with lots of dark fruit characters mixed with a roasted coffee and chocolate edge.

**QUADRUPLE**: The strongest of the Belgian Abbey styles, this beer is usually very dark with hints of raisin, liquorice, port and banana. Westvletern XII is the most famous of this style and is the so-called "best beer in the world." Supposedly, you can only get it at the gates of the Abbey, but there is a thriving grey market for it. Either way, we prefer Rochefort 10.

**RUSSIAN IMPERIAL STOUT**: Originally brewed for export to Russia (hence the name), this beer is a very, very strong version of a stout. Some say it had to be so strong to avoid freezing in Russia, but we think it was brewed so strong because it tastes delicious, especially after some time in a whisky barrel.

**SACCHRONOMYCES CEREVISIAE**: The scientific name for ale yeast, which ferments quickly on top of the beer.

**SACCHAROMYCES PASTORIANUS**: The scientific name for lager yeast, which ferments at the bottom of the beer and needs longer in the tank to round out the off-flavours it produces.

**SESSION BEER (OR SESSIONABLE BEER)**: We see it as a beer that can make you lose count of how many you have had but still lets you keep your breakfast down the next day. Should be low ABV, but still loaded with flavour.

**SESSION IPA**: Depending on where the beer is made, this may or may not actually be a low-strength IPA. In America, apparently a 5% beer can still be a session beer, which has caused many a British drinker to choke on his 3.5% pale ale. Either way, it's supposed to reduce the ABV while keeping that hoppy dominance.

**STOUT**: Originally called "stout porter," this style was simply a stronger porter. It has now come to mean a drier, more roasty dark beer with lots of heavily roasted malts.

**TRAPPIST BEER**: A Trappist beer must be brewed under the supervision of monks within the walls of a Trappist abbey with the profits going to the upkeep of the monastery or good causes. Without the usual commercial pressures, in some cases perfected over centuries, and showing an obsession with quality that only those with a lot of time on their hands can offer, many Trappist beers rank among the best in the world.

**TRIPEL**: Invented at Westmalle Abbey, whose beer is known as "the mother of triples," this beer is a strong, slightly hoppy, but yeast-forward blonde ale with lots of bready spice. It is usually lagered for months to clarify and smoothen.

**WEISSBIER**: I have yet to drink a weissbier not made in Munich that comes remotely close to the originals. Paulaner, Hacker-Pschorr, Weihenstephan and Schneideweiss all make truly beautiful examples, and there is no reason to deviate from these delicious, banana-y, clove-y and bubblegummy wheat beers. Fruity, velvety and cloudy, they are unlike any other beer style in the world and transport you to a Bavarian beer garden in one sip.

**WHITE WHALE**: The term used for a beer that makes beer nerds froth at the mouth with excitement. Usually released on just one day a year and greeted with queues of adoring fans who then lose their shit on the internet if they don't get any.

**WIT**: Often lumped in with weissbiers, Belgian wits are actually very different even if the first one ever was brewed in an attempt to emulate the delicious weissbiers of Bavaria. Usually made with fruity Belgian yeast, coriander and orange peel, it has a pithy bite but lots of sweetness and spice.

**WORT**: The beer before any fermentation has taken place, so essentially a malty hop tea. Add whisky and you have yourself a "brewer's breakfast."

**YEAST**: A happy little microbe whose only ambition is to make bread rise and beer alcoholic. It eats up sugar and poops out alcohol, carbon dioxide and delicious smelling esters, as well as lots of undesirable things it usually then gets rid of.

**ZYTHOPHILIA**: A love of all things beer, aka: what you have now.

# ACKNOWLEDGEMENTS

JONNY WOULD LIKE TO THANK

This book would not have been possible without the patience of my beautiful Heather and the talent of my main man Brad. I've also totally exploited the understanding and friendship of my colleagues at Cave, the expertise of Buxton Brewery's Colin Stronge and Malt Box's Will Longmate, the skills of Matt Curtis, guidance of Mark Dredge, and the steady hand of Sam Calvert. But the biggest thanks has to go to you guys for buying the book and watching the channel. Without you we'd be drunks without purpose. Now we're drunks with a book to justify it.

BRAD WOULD LIKE TO THANK

Jonny for being my partner in crime and sharing this crazy and exciting journey into the world of beer with me; my loving family George, Georgina and Steve who always told me to do what I love; my supportive girlfriend Melissa for putting up with me; and my father Terry, who was one of my best friends and one of the coolest guys you're ever likely meet. I miss him greatly every day.

# ABOUT THE AUTHORS

Jonny and Brad founded the Craft Beer Channel back in 2013 in a bid to get some free beers. Since then it has grown to become one of the world's biggest resources in information and stories about craft beer, with 10,000s of followers all over the world tuning in every week. They now travel the world making films, taking photos and writing about their experience so that people can enjoy their beers and time with friends more.

## JONNY GARRETT

Jonny is a beer expert, writer and now (apparently) filmmaker who has had a short but glittering career in blagging freebies. After an unsuccessful period of being a music journalist, and an even less successful stint as a real journalist, he got a job writing for Jamie Oliver as deputy editor of jamieoliver.com. It was there that his love of food, beer and YouTube collided and he's never looked back. He is now one of the UK's most recognisable beer experts, writing for national newspapers, magazines and now his own books.

# BRAD EVANS

A graduate of Central Saint Martin's School of Art and Design, Brad has spent over a decade working throughout the creative industries in London as a graphic designer, illustrator, art director, animator and branding expert. His clients have included the BBC, Channel 4, Jamie Oliver, Vice and MTV. With a love of adventure, travel and food, the burgeoning craft beer market in the UK resonated with his experiences in America and he launched the Craft Beer Channel with Jonny to hopefully become a part of the developing scene. Brad hopes to one day pack it all in and open up a cheeky little brew pub, where he can live the good life kicking out the jams and perfecting some stonking IPAs with his mates.

CPSIA information can be obtained
at www.ICGtesting.com
Printed in the USA
BVOW05s0305281016

466251BV00006B/6/P